ABOUT THE AUTHOR

DAVID ROBIE was awarded New Zealand's 1985 Media Peace Prize for his reporting of the voyage of the *Rainbow Warrior* to the Marshall Islands and the sabotage. He was one of the few journalists to accompany the campaigners and spent 11 weeks on board.

Previously he has lived in Australia, Africa and France for a number of years. He has been editor or held senior editorial posts on several newspapers, including the *Sunday Observer* (Melbourne) and *Rand Daily Mail* (Johannesburg). In recent years he has covered South Pacific affairs as a freelance writer. His articles appear in several publications, including *Islands Business* news magazine and the *New Zealand Times*. When he isn't travelling the South Pacific or beachcombing, he is often found in the Waiwhiu Valley, Northland, where he has a share in a cooperative farm.

EYES *of* FIRE

The Last Voyage of the *Rainbow Warrior*

David Robie

FOREWORD BY WALTER LINI

PUBLISHED IN COOPERATION WITH
GREENPEACE

new society publishers

Philadelphia, Pennsylvania

To Lucien and Simeon,
who were lucky not to be on board the night of the bombing.

Inquiries about requests to republish all or part of the materials contained herein
should be addressed to:
  New Society Publishers
  4722 Baltimore Avenue
  Philadelphia, PA 19143

ISBN: Hardcover 0-86571-113-5
ISBN: Paperback 0-86571-114-3

First published in 1986 by:
  Lindon Publishing
  P.O. Box 39-225
  Auckland West, New Zealand

Part of the royalties of this book go to the Rongelap Resettlement Fund.

Maps by Dexter Fry
Design by Phillip Ridge

For more information about Greenpeace, write:
  Greenpeace
  1611 Connecticut Avenue NW
  Washington, DC 20009

New Society Publishers is a project of the New Society Educational Foundation
and a collective of the Movement for a New Society. New Society Educational
Foundation is a nonprofit, tax-exempt, public foundation. Movement for a New
Society is a network of small groups and individuals working for fundamental
social change through nonviolent action. To learn more about MNS, write:
Movement for a New Society, PO Box 1922, Cambridge, MA 02238. Opinions
expressed in this book do not necessarily represent positions of either New
Society Educational Foundation or Movement for a New Society.

Cover photograph by John Miller. Frontispiece photograph by Gil Hanly.
Contents page photograph of Fernando Pereira by David Robie.

CONTENTS

Thanks to Robert Hunter and Peter Willcox, for the inspiration, somewhere west of Johnston Atoll. Thanks to David McTaggart, Steve Sawyer, Carol Stewart and Elaine Shaw, for their patience and time amid such stress. Thanks to Davey Edward and Lloyd Anderson, for their Breakfast Club sustenance and encouragement. Thanks to Julian Riklon, Lijon Eknilang and Charles Rara, for hardening my resolve to record the devastation wrought on Pacific islanders by nuclear testing. Thanks to Giff Johnson, Glenn Alcalay, Peter Hayes, and Marie-Thérèse and Dr Bengt Danielsson for their research. Thanks to Hilary Anderson, Bunny McDiarmid, Margaret Mills, John Miller, Gil Hanly, Jann O'Keefe, Chris Robinson and Ursula Kortner for their support. Thanks to Waterfall Farm Co-operative, Waiwhiu Valley, for the tranquillity needed. And thanks to all those I haven't named who also helped.

My appreciation also to Greenpeace for their help.

The photographs are mine except where otherwise credited.

Foreword

I FIRST heard of the plan to bring the international ecology group Greenpeace's flagship, *Rainbow Warrior*, to the Pacific when I made a visit to the movement's Auckland office in December 1984, after having participated in a meeting of the South Pacific Forum ministerial group on New Caledonia in Wellington. I was asked whether the government of Vanuatu would give its approval for the *Rainbow Warrior* to visit Vanuatu, after her humanitarian mission in the Marshall Islands, and before she left via New Zealand to Moruroa Atoll to protest against the continued French nuclear tests there. I told Greenpeace officials that not only would we approve of the visit, but that the government and people of Vanuatu would be honoured to welcome the *Rainbow Warrior* and her crew.

Six months later, on the morning of 27 June 1985, we had the great pleasure of welcoming the *Rainbow Warrior* into nuclear-free Port Vila. I went out on a government vessel with most of my cabinet ministers to welcome and escort the *Rainbow Warrior* and her crew into the harbour. The next day, I had a meeting with a delegation from the ship. In the evening, I hosted on behalf of the government a reception in honour of the visit of the *Rainbow Warrior* and her crew. I told them they faced danger from the French Navy and that I admired their courage for what they were doing for humanity. But I did not know at the time that about two weeks later their ship would be brutally blown up and sunk in Auckland harbour by terrorist bombs which caused the death of one crew member, Fernando Pereira. I was shocked on hearing the sad news. It was a miracle that our official, Charles Rara, who accompanied the crew of the *Rainbow Warrior* when they sailed from Port Vila, was at the time ashore visiting friends. Otherwise he could also have been a victim because he was sharing the cabin with Pereira.

My government decided to accord official welcome to the *Rainbow Warrior* to highlight the fact that there are nuclear-free nations in the Pacific as well as countries which are being used by outside powers to test their nuclear devices in the region. I believe that in order effectively to oppose and protest against either the continued testing of nuclear devices or the maintenance of colonial outposts in our region, all our governments — especially those comprising the Forum — should work more closely with non-governmental organisations and other groups such as anti-nuclear campaigners, independence movements, environmental groups, trade unions, religious organisations, sympathetic news media as well as universities and student associations.

It is becoming more evident in our region that a lot of governments prefer not to listen to the views of these various groups, particularly on the nuclear and decolonisation issues. However, some governments are only too happy to exploit these two issues as mere public relations exercises to gain public support during election time. Once they get voted into power these two issues take back seats in terms of priority.

Some governments even go to the extent of labelling some of these groups as communist-inspired. We in Vanuatu do not think this is so and we are prepared to work closely with them to achieve our common objective of an independent and nuclear-free Pacific.

I have always maintained that colonialism and nuclearism in the Pacific are part of the same evil. To eradicate this evil from our region I believe that we have to deal with it from its root, which is colonialism itself. It is morally wrong for an alien power to occupy someone else's territory, suppress its people and use that territory's environment to test deadly weapons. Unless French Polynesia becomes independent France will continue to use it to test its nuclear bombs. Now the French Government is more determined than ever to maintain its control of French Polynesia. This is clearly shown by the bombing of the *Rainbow Warrior* — carried out by its agents from the Direction Générale de la Sécurité Extérieure (DGSE) — and by the visits to Moruroa by President Mitterrand and Prime Minister Fabius in September and October 1985.

The same is true of the Marshall Islands. As long as they remain under the armpit of the United States their environment will continue to be exploited for nuclear programmes and their people exposed to nuclear contamination. I believe that complete decolonisation of the Pacific, coupled with more regional governments sympathetic to mass opinion on the independence and nuclear issues, would inevitably bring about denuclearisation of the region.

David Robie was the only journalist on board the *Rainbow Warrior* when she left Port Vila for Auckland where she was put out of action by the DGSE agents. He was on board for 11 weeks, covering the evacuation of the fallout-ravaged people of Rongelap Atoll in the Marshall Islands. Thus he is well placed to provide us with this vivid account of the *Rainbow Warrior's* last voyage and the connection of Rongelap and Moruroa with colonialism in the Pacific.

WALTER H. LINI
Prime Minister
Republic of Vanuatu

CHAPTER ONE

How Sir William became the Warrior

She was a worker; she would give her guts and she would ride out any storm. But most of all the Rainbow Warrior *had a special, elusive quality.*
— Cook Hilary Anderson

GREENPEACE'S eco-navy was born in the Pacific. A cosy little 'floating farmhouse' called the *Phyllis Cormack* set sail in mid-September 1971 from Vancouver bound for the Aleutian Islands in the North Pacific. On board were a motley collection of Canadian ecologists, journalists, lawyers, hippies and a draft-dodging energy researcher. Chartered by the Don't Make a Wave Committee, which later became the Greenpeace Foundation, the rusty 25-metre halibut-seiner headed towards Amchitka Island in a brave attempt to prevent a five-megaton nuclear test by the United States on the windswept wildlife sanctuary.

As a protest, the voyage was a failure. The blast went ahead before the ship got there. But as a public relations campaign it was a brilliant success and the Atomic Energy Commission abandoned the rest of the series.

The following year, the focus moved to the South Pacific. In April, an 11-metre New Zealand-built ketch, *Vega*, departed from Auckland for Moruroa Atoll to protest against the detonation of French nuclear bombs slung from helium-filled balloons.[1] The yacht was skippered and owned by David McTaggart, a 39-year-old Canadian construction industry millionaire who had lost his fortune. After playing cat-and-mouse with the French Navy, the *Vega* was rammed by a French minesweeper and left paralysed on the high seas before being towed to Moruroa for makeshift repairs.

The yacht made another protest against French tests in 1973, this time accompanied by several yachts, including the *Fri* and *Spirit of Peace*, and a New Zealand Navy frigate, *Otago*. But the *Vega* was the last of the 'peace boats' to remain in the test zone and a French warship sent a Zodiac inflatable speedboat with commandos armed with truncheons to deal with her.

Photographs and news of the brutal beating up of McTaggart and English crewman Nigel Ingram made world headlines. The protests and a lawsuit by New Zealand against France in the International Court of Justice at The Hague forced Paris to abandon atmospheric blasts the following year and they began underground testing in 1975 at Moruroa and the neighbouring atoll of Fangataufa.

Greenpeace had scored two early environmental successes — both in the Pacific. As the popularity of the fledgling ecology movement swelled, small groups were begun in several countries in a loose coalition under the Greenpeace banner. Campaigning spread from nuclear tests to other conservation issues. The 'human barrier' technique was developed as Greenpeace inflatable speedboat crews defied harpoons, forcing Soviet whaling fleets to abandon operations off California. In anti-sealing campaigns on the Labrador Ice Pack, protesters risked arrest and being plunged into icy water to save snow-white pups from being clubbed to death for the fur trade.

The philosophy of non-violent, direct action emerged as a powerful weapon for conservation. Life had to be saved by what the Quakers call 'bearing witness'. A person bearing witness must accept responsibility for being aware of an injustice. That person may then choose to do something or stand by but may not turn away in 'feigned' ignorance. The Greenpeace ethic is not only to bear witness personally to atrocities against life, it is to take direct action to prevent them. Although action must be direct it must also be non-violent.

By the end of 1977 another ship joined the Greenpeace fleet, heralding a new era for the movement. Called *Sir William Hardy*, she was a 49-metre, 22-berth North Sea fisheries research vessel built in Aberdeen, Scotland, during 1956 for the British Government. Rusting, ignored in London's East India Docks, she had outlived her usefulness as a research ship. Armed with a grant of £40,000 from the Dutch branch of the World Wildlife Fund, David McTaggart bought the ship for Greenpeace Europe. She was christened *Rainbow Warrior*.

One of the people originally involved with the *Rainbow Warrior*, Remi Parmentier, who ran the Greenpeace France office in Paris, suggested the name, or at least a Gallic version, *Le Combattant de l'Arc-en-ciel*. He was prompted by the French writer Hugo Verlomme, author of the marine fantasy novel *Mer-mère* about dolphins. But, argued Susi Newborn, a founder of Greenpeace UK, the French was too much of a mouthful. Better to stick with the English. (Two years later in 1979 the book *Warriors of the Rainbow* was published, a chronicle of early Greenpeace campaigns written by former president Robert Hunter, which told about the Cree prophecies of the ecological disasters that would befall the human race if nature was not respected. Subsequently, the myth grew that the book's title had influenced the naming of the ship; chronology was, however, against it.)

The *Rainbow Warrior* was the first big campaign ship actually owned by Greenpeace — all the others had been charter boats or on loan. She naturally became the flagship of a fleet which eventually included several other large boats such as the trawler *Cedarlea*, the pilot boat *Sirius*, the riverboat *Beluga* and an ocean-going tug, *Greenpeace*, bought in 1985 to establish the world's first base camp set up by a private group in the Antarctic.

The 'R Dub' had a colourful life — campaigns against whaling by Iceland, Peru, Spain and the Soviet Union;

combating radioactive waste dumping by the British freighter *Gem*; a dramatic escape from military arrest in the Spanish port of El Ferrol; and the seizure of seven crewmembers at gunpoint by Russian soldiers on the Siberian coast while documenting illegal Soviet whaling. Most of the campaigns were waged in European or North American waters.

The year 1985 was planned to be the Year of the Pacific. The *Rainbow Warrior* set off on a year-long voyage with the initial task of evacuating 320 Marshall Islanders from Rongelap Atoll, ravaged by fallout from United States' nuclear tests 31 years earlier. She then visited the bastions of a nuclear-free Pacific, Vanuatu and New Zealand. The *Warrior* was also to have led a protest flotilla to Moruroa. But three days after arriving in Auckland Harbour, just before midnight on 10 July, two bombs placed by the French secret service sank the ship and crewman Fernando Pereira drowned.

The death of Pereira and the violation of New Zealand's sovereignty by a 'friendly' nation touched off an international furore. Greenpeace, proud of a record of never having lost a life, or even suffering any serious injuries in 14 years of peaceful but frequently hazardous campaigning, had become a target for state-backed terrorism.

French Prime Minister Laurent Fabius admitted two months after the bombing that the *Rainbow Warrior* had been sunk on orders by the Direction Générale de la Sécurité Extérieure, France's secret service. The admission, following the resignation of the Defence Minister, Charles Hernu, and the sacking of DGSE chief Admiral Pierre Lacoste, was as threatening to the socialist government of President Mitterrand as the Bokassa diamonds scandal was to his conservative predecessor, Giscard d'Estaing.

Greenpeace leaders feared international intrigue might taint its peaceful philosophy and rejection of partisan politics. But a wave of sympathy and support in New Zealand and other countries eased their fears.

Back in 1977, there were no such problems. Greenpeace then was a vaguely anarchistic collection of national groups waging a clean, open 'war' on ecological issues.

Susi Newborn, a 27-year-old publisher and activist, cleaning firm manager Denise Bell, 35, Charles Hutchinson and Alan Thornton, a Canadian Greenpeace member steeped in Cree Indian lore, had set up the British head-quarters in a tiny office off Trafalgar Square with £200 saved from selling 'Save-the-Whales' T-shirts. They had a dream of buying a trawler to save the whales in the North Atlantic and when they heard of a trawler for sale in the East India Docks they went down to inspect her. Newborn stood on the bridge with Bell and all they could see was a heap of rust in a filthy basin.

'She looks great,' said Bell. 'Let's buy her!'

The World Wildlife Fund provided the money three months later. Bell and Newborn called for volunteers to help get the *Rainbow Warrior* seaworthy and about 20 people came to help chip away rust and paint her by hand.

Australian Chris Robinson, a 25-year-old former

lifeguard from Port Albert, Victoria, joined the volunteers. He was living in a Stratford community house with eight people — including Newborn — at the time and he didn't know anything about painting a ship. But he agreed to take on the job and started from the bow. Seven coats of paint; it seemed an impossible task.

Then someone thought of using a compressor and needle guns. Now the job appeared more realistic. Some days there were as many as 25 people with hammers chipping on deck. Her hull was painted dark green with a rainbow and a white dove bearing an olive branch.

Work began on overhauling the engines. A couple of Bell's friends, two tough characters who did demolition work for a living, hacked off a big fishing winch on the main deck left over from her side-trawling days. Tony Marriner organised the marine gear, inflatable boats and survival suits.

The volunteers worked for three gruelling months to transform the *Rainbow Warrior* into a proud campaign ship. The wheelhouse was rather lumpy and unattractive, but the rest of her was appealing. She had a high North Sea bow, graceful sheerline and round-the-corner stern.

Eager to shed the amateur image of earlier campaign voyages in North America, British Greenpeace advertised for experienced merchant seamen and engineers interested in conservation. Black-bearded Nick Hill, an easy-going master off the *Oil Hunter*, a seismic survey ship in the North Sea, became skipper. Chief mate Alastair Hamilton had a master's ocean-going ticket as well, and Peter 'Bogey'

Bouquet had been second mate on a coastal tanker. Another experienced mate, Jon Castle, who later became skipper, was left out of the crew at this stage — there wasn't room for him.

Dutchman Simon Hollander was an outstanding engineer and so was Tim Mark, a second engineer from a P & O liner. Athel 'Ace' von Koettlitz also had engineering skills and eventually became Greenpeace's technical director.

Ship's cook Hilary Anderson, a 29-year-old New Zealander, had been a French teacher before becoming a chef at the vegetarian restaurant Food for Thought near Covent Garden. Her first job on board was to paint the galley.

The fourth woman crewmember was Sally Austin, 31, who left a decade of nursing and her beloved Devon countryside to join the *Warrior*.

It was touch and go to complete paperwork with the Board of Trade before the *Rainbow Warrior* left on her maiden voyage as an ecology vessel. A 'ship's passport', a certificate registering her new name and change of status from research ship to pleasure boat — the only appropriate category — was needed. But the name had to be permanently etched on to the ship. At the last moment before leaving London, Tony Marriner chalked out 'Rainbow Warrior' on the stern and bow, drilling holes marking the letters.

As the ship left port on 1 May for a trial run, mocking dockers lined the waterfront.

'Yer not going to sea in that thing, are yer?' they jeered.

The first trip was just north of Dunbar, Scotland, where a big rally was being staged in opposition to the Torness advanced gas-cooled nuclear reactor. On board was David McTaggart, now director of Greenpeace Europe. Although not keen on public speaking, McTaggart made an impassioned address to the crowd.

For the first time, the crew had a good opportunity to train themselves in the use of Zodiac and Avon inflatable speedboats in preparation for an anti-whaling campaign in Iceland.

'It's dead easy . . . just like driving a big trail bike,' said McTaggart, but one of the boats was punctured while carrying a wind-powered generator ashore — brought to illustrate the advantages of natural power.

After a European tour, the *Rainbow Warrior* began her ecological campaign in June 1978. A handful of wellwishers farewelled her from Lerwick in the Shetland Islands as she set out to challenge an Icelandic whaling fleet in the North Atlantic. Since before the time of the Vikings, the Icelanders had been hunting whales and almost everything else that lives in the sea. Their right to harvest whales had never before been challenged.

Iceland was chosen as a target because it continued to hunt fin whales. The fin was a protected species in all seas except for the North Atlantic where Iceland, Spain and whaling pirates continued to hunt them. Furthermore, Iceland was a consistent supporter of Japan and the Soviet Union on crucial votes within the International Whaling Commission forum, and continued to trade in whale products with Japan. In 1972 Iceland supported a 10-year moratorium on commercial whaling at a United Nations Environmental Conference in Stockholm. Two weeks later it opposed the moratorium being put to the IWC vote. The following year the moratorium was again on the agenda and failed by one vote; Iceland rejected the measure that could have saved more than 200,000 great whales which have since been slaughtered.

On the way to stalking the fin whaling fleet, countless meetings were held on board to plan campaign tactics. Fred Easton had filmed near California a 100-kilogram explosive harpoon darting over the heads of two Greenpeace campaigners in a Zodiac and exploding in a whale. As well as adopting the human barrier approach, the *Warrior* crew were determined to wage the campaign in their own style and Easton had little influence.

Alastair Hamilton wanted military-like precision with the inflatable boats and he demanded constant practice to develop split-second timing. Manual winching gear on the boat deck was used to launch and pick up the boats while almost at full speed. The boats would zip between an imaginary harpoon and whale and then be hauled back on deck.

Two Avons, inflatables with steering wheels rather than tillers, had been obtained in the Shetlands to join the Zodiacs.

The crew were still settling in. Nick Hill's conventional maritime background made him ill-at-ease with the women crew. At first, he was particularly wary of the vegetarian cooking of Hilary Anderson and he would wander into the galley, sniffing and suspiciously lifting cookpot lids. But he got used to it. Parmentier, a gifted organiser but no sailor, often curled up like a mouse in the messroom. Hollander's gruffness was sometimes irritating. McTaggart kept a chocolate cache in the drawer under his bunk.

Finding the whalers was hard going. Many nights were spent on watch in the crow's nest, braced against the bitter cold. Everybody was involved in whaler-spotting with the radar.

The first whaler they tracked down, with the help of eavesdropping on the radio, emerged out of the mist with one whale lashed to the side and was hunting another one.

'That bloody little green devil box is on our tail,' said the Icelandic radio operator.

Four inflatable boats were launched. As they were lowered, Anderson leant over the side of the *Warrior* and tossed three Mars bars in each for good luck. She had a secret stash of them.

Chris Robinson, driving the leading boat, and Charles Hutchinson ploughed into heavy seas. The swell was so big that the *Rainbow Warrior* kept vanishing from sight. Robinson managed to get in front of the whaler which was dicey because the whale it was chasing was tiring, and was breaking the surface a lot and gasping for air. It was a long chase and when the other inflatables got close they ran into problems, engine trouble or crew getting hurt by the heavy buffeting from the sea.

'This is as rough as guts,' said Robinson, as Hutchinson sprawled at the bottom of the boat and the whaler bore down on them. A seaman aimed the harpoon gun, trying to line up the whale. Shivers went down Robinson's spine. Was he going to shoot?

But the seaman couldn't get a clear shot at the whale and the whaler was forced to give up the hunt and return to Hvalfjördur (ford of the whales). Icelandic law required whalers to return to port with a catch within 20 hours. The Icelandic coast guard, recently involved in the Cod War with Britain, did not intervene during the campaign.

The *Rainbow Warrior* put into the capital, Reykjavik, and the crew addressed public meetings, having turned the whaling issue into a national controversy for the first time. Some crew slipped into a whaling station at Hvalfjördur, 160 kilometres north of Reykjavik, for a visit. An unsuspecting hunter was asked if he thought whales felt pain when he fired explosive harpoons into them.

'Hell yes, they'll scream like a pig if you don't get them in the heart with your first shot,' he replied.

There were some changes to the *Warrior's* crew at this time. Hamilton, who couldn't quite get used to a crew which didn't have a real hierarchy, had left the ship by the time the *Warrior* reached Iceland and Jon Castle took his place. Denise Bell needed to return to London; the office was falling apart without her managing skills. About this time Greenpeace gained truck driver Peter Wilkinson, of the Friends of the Earth, who eventually became director of Greenpeace UK.

The *Warrior* refuelled in Dublin in July and launched a campaign against the UK Atomic Energy Authority freighter *Gem* which was dumping barrels of radioactive waste about 560 kilometres offshore in the Bay of Biscay. Zodiac crews sped alongside the ship in an attempt to prevent the dumping of the barrels. One 300-kilogram barrel slammed into an inflatable driven by Athel von Koettlitz. It damaged the boat but he wasn't injured.

Film and photographs of the incident exposed the issue to the world. Newspapers and television covered the campaign in detail in Austria and a referendum there rejected plans to commission the country's first nuclear reactor. The *Warrior* staged one more anti-dumping campaign and the *Sirius* two over the next four years before forcing a halt.

In August she sailed to north-west Spain where whales had been slaughtered since the eighth century. Since Spain was not a member of the IWC it was not commonly known that a company in the province of Galicia was still whaling. Spain had supported the 10-year moratorium but Industria Ballenera SA, owned by millionaire Júan Masso and his family, were operating four whalers. Two whaling stations were in use south of La Coruña.

For three days the *Rainbow Warrior* prevented a whaler from hunting despite the presence of two Spanish corvettes The corvettes disappeared but when the *Warrior* shadowed the whaler into the port of La Coruña, navy officers on board a pilot boat ordered her to tie up alongside the dock. Hilary Anderson noted:

Fearing to lose our ship — bought with public money — in a web of Spanish bureaucracy, our crew stalled any decision to comply with naval orders until their legal position had been clarified. The Spanish authorities decided to go ashore at night to consult their higher authorities. As the pilot boat disappeared behind the breakwater, the lights of the *Rainbow Warrior* were quickly turned off, the anchor hauled up and the course set for Portugal. Ironically, this day was the 400th anniversary of the defeat of the Spanish Armada.

The skipper of the *Rainbow Warrior* was publicly outlawed for refusing to obey Spanish naval orders. But ecologists throughout the world regarded the Masso brothers as the real outlaws for defying IWC whaling rules.

A month later the *Warrior* sailed for the Orkney Islands on the Scottish Coast to protect almost 4,000 grey seals from slaughter. The crew staged a nine-day protest against the Norwegian sealing ship *Kvitungen* which resulted in the Scottish Office calling a one-year moratorium on seal killing.

Jon Castle, a man of stern principles, gave a glimpse here of the idealism that later marked his captaincy. A crew needed to be put ashore on Rona Island to defend the seals but the safest landing spot on the rugged shoreline was in the middle of a colony. Castle refused to let the boat land there and disturb the seals. Instead, he insisted upon making the landing at a far more treacherous place along the coast.

Iceland refused to support a motion proposed by the

Seychelles IWC calling for a three-year ban on the killing of sperm whales. So during 1979 the *Rainbow Warrior* headed for Reykjavik on another anti-whaling campaign. This time the Icelandic coast guard was ready. However, the *Warrior* also had on board a 'secret weapon' — an RI-28, a high-speed 10-metre fibreglass boat capable of 50 knots, which could cruise for up to 12 hours.

For several days, the *Warrior* and her fleet of inflatables lay in wait outside Reykjavik for the whalers. Richard Kenna was camped ashore on a peak overlooking the harbour and briefed the ship by radio.

On 15 June the captain of an Icelandic whaler, *Hvalur 8*, fired five harpoons over the heads of Greenpeace campaigners trying to protect a 12-metre fin whale. One harpoon exploded into the whale only five metres from the nearest protester and blood surged into the sea. The RI-28 was damaged during the confrontation and was towed into Reykjavik for repairs. While the *Warrior* stocked up on supplies and fuel, Icelandic authorities took action against skipper Peter Bouquet.

'You all know that the police came on board today,' McTaggart told the crew that evening. 'Peter was called into court and we have simply been served with a piece of paper. It's not a writ, it's a complaint by the whaler, Larson, regarding the harassment of his boats.

'The judge asked Peter and I to appear in court tomorrow at 1 o'clock. If we leave tonight before the court hearing and harass the whalers we're not up for a jail sentence because we do not have an injunction in our hands.

It is the opinion of the few of us who have been talking to the lawyer for the last few hours that we should leave right now.'

Heading out to sea once again in search of the whaling fleet, the *Warrior* was confronted by an Icelandic frigate. The radio crackled into life.

Warship: *Rainbow Warrior*, I have a message for your captain. Are you ready?

McTaggart: Yes we are, go ahead.

Warship: We have orders to tell you to go back to Reykjavik, where the court has asked you to stay

McTaggart: We have one question: Are we under arrest?

Warship: One moment please.

Minutes later, the answer came: Rainbow Warrior, you are under arrest.

McTaggart replied he would call back shortly. 'Now what?' he asked. After a brief crew meeting, he called the frigate: 'We have discussed it here on the *Rainbow Warrior*. We are totally in opposition to your arresting us. But we respect your laws, your rights and your territorial waters and we will return to Reykjavik as long as you enter into your log that we are returning under protest.'

Despite the arrest, the *Rainbow Warrior* kept dogging the whalers for more than six weeks.

Right: *The RI-28 fibreglass boat was used effectively in the 1979 Icelandic and 1980 Spanish whaling campaigns. Its hull is surrounded by a large rubber tube for added buoyancy. With a full load of petrol it could travel 1600 kilometres and be independent of the* Rainbow Warrior. *(Greenpeace)*

By January 1980 the *Warrior* was at Guernsey, the home of Jon Castle, now the skipper. They were waiting for the *Pacific Swan*, a freighter carrying highly radioactive fuel rods from Japan to the reprocessing plants of La Hague, near the French port of Cherbourg, and Windscale in Britain. Reprocessing involves stripping plutonium from spent fuel rods and is one of the most dangerous processes in the nuclear fuel cycle.

American Steve Sawyer, a 23-year-old philosophy graduate from Haverford College in Philadelphia, had joined the crew. The year before he had been involved in the Clamshell Alliance campaign to occupy the Seabrook nuclear power plant, 100 kilometres north of Boston, just across the New Hampshire border. The huge alliance could have succeeded if the movement had not rejected 'organisation'.

Sawyer learned a lot then. He rapidly developed an astuteness and organisational ability which belied his age. He was also a serious man with a caustic wit who carried around 'Environmental Extremist' business cards for fun.

Waiting for the *Pacific Swan* to arrive, Sawyer made contact with the French activist group CCPAH, Committee Contre la Pollution Atomique dans la Hague. French protesters, including the mayor of La Hague village, sailed for Guernsey and joined the *Rainbow Warrior* crew. They kept a 24-hour watch for the freighter.

Just after midnight on St Valentine's Day the *Warrior* was patrolling outside the French 12-mile limit, with a French cruiser shadowing them just inside the limit, when a radio request by the *Pacific Swan* for a pilot was intercepted. The *Warrior* dashed at full speed, 12 knots, through the fog for Cherbourg. The cruiser tailed her, flashing a spotlight until she was six kilometres from port. Two tugs and a minesweeper guarded the narrow entrance to the harbour.

The *Rainbow Warrior* was warned to stop. But Castle faked a starboard turn and instead went to the port side, trying to slip through the boats into the harbour. One of the tugs rammed the side of the *Warrior* smashing stanchions under the boat deck. As the ship ploughed towards the dock Castle went full astern, but the bow hit, flattening the steel plates.

About 50 riot police armed with rifles, bayonets and grappling hooks lined the dockside and seized the *Warrior* just before dawn. But hundreds of French anti-nuclear protesters were also there. Cannisters of spent fuel rods unloaded from the *Pacific Swan* were to be transported by rail to the La Hague reprocessing plant about 16 kilometres away and protesters blocked the line. When riot police turned high pressure hoses on them, the water scoured out the railway tracks. Headlines in next morning's French press mocked: 'Greenpeace Makes Fools Of French Navy'. The incident probably contributed heavily to the undying hostility the French Navy has towards the ecology movement.

Next day the authorities ordered the *Rainbow Warrior* out of France, escorting her out of the harbour and banning her from returning.

Sawyer was asked by McTaggart to return to Boston. Greenpeace USA was in a mess and it took him about six months to sort out the $1 million-a-year corporation's problems.

On board the *Rainbow Warrior* now was 'Martini' Gotje, a 29-year-old lean Dutchman. As a new immigrant to New Zealand from the Dutch merchant navy in 1973, he had joined the *Fri* on the protest voyage to Moruroa and continued on a round-the-world peace crusade lasting seven years.

Back in Spain, the Masso whaling company had continued an unrestricted slaughter. Spain still failed to supply scientific data on the whale kill or the state of whale stocks, and refused to support any IWC preservation proposals.

But tension was high in Galicia. Two of the four Spanish whalers had been sabotaged during April in the port of Marin, near Pontevedra. Greenpeace was blamed by Industria Ballenera SA while the news media rejected the accusation. The following month Remi Parmentier and a photographer were arrested for trespassing at one of the whale stations which they wanted to photograph. Police also broke up a 'Salvad Las Ballenas' (Save the Whales) demonstration in La Coruña.

The *Rainbow Warrior* left Portugal on 14 June with two television crews, radio and magazine journalists on board, plus the bright-orange RI-28. It was hoped to keep the 'outlawed' ship away from the Spanish whaling fleet and rely on the speed of the RI-28.

Four days later, they found the *Ibsa Tres*, one of the last two remaining Spanish whalers near Vigo. The whaler stopped and a handwritten message was delivered to the captain in a Zodiac. When the whaler crew refused to accept the message, one of the campaigners tossed it on board. The letter said the crew of the *Rainbow Warrior* represented nine nationalities and millions of people throughout the world, and they appealed to the seamen to stop killing whales before it was too late.

A Spanish corvette, *Cardaso*, arrived but failed to deter the *Warrior* from harassing the whaler. Radio operator Mark Long recorded the scene:

> It was an amazing sight: The *Ibsa Tres* churning through the Atlantic intent on finding whales; the Greenpeace Zodiacs manoeuvring at high speeds about the whaler; the *Rainbow Warrior* following close behind; and the Spanish warship circling ever closer into the midst of the action.

A pod of whales was sighted. Although the *Cardaso* cut across her bows, the *Warrior* ignored the warning and continued to thwart the *Ibsa Tres* in her whaling attempts. Finally, the whaler gave up — and waited.

On the horizon, a second corvette, *H.V. Pinzon*, appeared. Drawing closer, the commander ordered the *Warrior* to accept a boarding party.

'No,' Gotje snorted.

A fin whale surfaced near the *Rainbow Warrior* and the crew of the *Ibsa Tres* manned the harpoon gun. Jon

Castle skilfully played 'dodgem' with both the whaler and the *Cardaso*, narrowly missing the corvette in a collision which could have torn a hole in the more lightly built warship.

The whaler was ordered back to shore, and the *H.V. Pinzon* again warned the *Warrior* she was about to be boarded. Not wanting to jeopardise the safety of the ship, Castle accepted, even though the arrest was in international waters. Under armed guard and the escort of both corvettes, the protest ship headed to the naval base of El Ferrol. On arrival, marines entered the engineroom and removed the main thrust bearing from the propulsion system to prevent an escape. Castle was taken away under guard for questioning.

El Ferrol was the birthplace of El Caudillo — General-issimo Franco, the fascist dictator who had ruled Spain for more than 35 years. Along with Barcelona and Cadiz it was one of Spain's three chief naval bases. But it turned out not to be as secure a fortress port as it was portrayed.

The television crews were sitting on a hot story, but the military judge was preventing them from getting their film out. Could it be smuggled? One press reporter had an idea. She hid some of the best film in the bottom of her suitcase under her knickers. When the guards opened the case and began rummaging, she feigned acute embarrassment. Red-faced, the guard hurriedly shut the case and let her leave.

Over the next few days the spectacular film was shown on television in more than 70 countries.

Crew members put up banners on the *Warrior* proclaiming 'Libertad Para Del Rainbow Warrior' and the number of days the ship had been detained. They refused to remove them and police boarded the ship to tear them down. When local townsfolk demonstrated in support of Greenpeace, the police made a baton-charge at them.

Months passed. Parts for the RI-28 arrived and the crew repaired the speedboat. Police were told the boat needed to be test-driven around the port. Instead, Athel von Koettlitz, New Zealander Bruce Crammond and Chris Robinson escaped and dashed more than 1,300 kilometres to attend the IWC meeting in Brighton. They made it as far as Jersey and then developed engine trouble, robbing them of the chance to address the meeting.

Castle told the angry judge the crew had slipped across to France for a 'holiday'.

Meanwhile, Robinson and von Koettlitz were trying to get new propulsion parts made up from the ship's blueprints to enable the *Warrior* to escape. There was little choice. Spanish authorities were ignoring pleas by the ecology movement's lawyers to have the ship released on the grounds that her capture was in violation of both international and Spanish law.

By November the pair had 100 kilograms of propulsion

Right: *Greenpeace campaigners and a journalist visited the Spanish whaler* Ibsa Tres *in 1980. The captain showed them catch figures and admitted that his own daughter did not approve of whaling. As the Greenpeace members left in Zodiacs a second warship arrived.* (Pierre Gleizes/Greenpeace)

parts, smuggled into Spain in a washing basket in an old Kombi van. Getting the parts on board was a problem. Several crew went to a nearby bar in the van, pretended to get drunk and returned to the ship. Chris Robinson was driver. Von Koettlitz, Tim Mark and Pierre Gleizes reeled on board, each clutching one of the parts, and the guards didn't notice anything.

McTaggart also smuggled himself on board and after the thrust bearing was fitted and working, the crew decided to make their escape about 10 p.m. on Saturday, 8 November. That evening, three of the four guards slipped off to a party.

'Brilliant,' thought McTaggart, who was keeping watch from the wheelhouse. It was 8 o'clock and already dark when he noticed the other guard leave as well. He called Castle:

'Hey, they've just one guard there and he's gone too,' McTaggart said. 'This is it Jon . . . it's time to go.'

Gleizes cut one mooring rope and Robinson, in the middle of cooking dinner, slipped another and they were away — two hours early. The *Warrior* headed out to sea at full steam, but marine growth on her hull after five months under arrest slowed her down. She couldn't muster anything more than six or seven knots.

But the crew needn't have worried. They made the

Left: *Spanish marine guards seen from the porthole of* Rainbow Warrior. *The ship was held under arrest in the naval base of El Ferrol for five months before its dramatic escape to Guernsey.* (Pierre Gleizes/Greenpeace)

voyage to Guernsey undisturbed. Two searching warships and navy helicopters called in to help at dawn the next day failed to find any sign of the *Warrior*.

Greenpeace was growing fast. By 1984 it had become multinational with almost 1.5 million members in 15 countries — Australia, Austria, Belgium, Britain, Canada, Denmark, France, Luxembourg, Netherlands, New Zealand, Spain, Sweden, Switzerland, United States and West Germany. The movement evolved as it had begun, with a great deal of autonomy at both national and international levels. But to keep pace with the growth, the international organisation needed to be streamlined. Greenpeace International had been formed in 1979 by Greenpeace Europe and the North American branches which had settled a drawn-out lawsuit. A 15-member world council had been set up with five international directors, including chairman David McTaggart.

Greenpeace Ltd, the British parent company, employed at least 10 paid office staff at its Islington headquarters in north London. Income, raised by private donations, occasional grants from other voluntary groups like the World Wildlife Fund, and sales from T-shirts and other merchandise, was growing. It reached $9 million a year worldwide by 1984. The worldwide campaign budget was about $1.8 million with $300,000 needed to run the international headquarters in Lewes, Britain.

The *Rainbow Warrior* needed more sophisticated protection from injunctions and other legal attempts to 'shut Greenpeace up and shut her down'. Originally, the ship was owned and operated by Greenpeace Ltd. In 1981 the legal ownership was changed to Rainbow Warrior Holdings Ltd, but two years later the ship was registered under Galleas Ltd, a company in the Cayman Islands. Rainbow Warrior Holdings remained as the management group for Greenpeace's eco-navy.

Towards the end of 1980 Steve Sawyer took a long break from Greenpeace, camping at his woodlands retreat near Boston. He rebuilt his pickup truck and then worked for an alternative energy company in Boston, making wind generators and smokeless wood-fired stoves.

A phone call came from McTaggart. The *Rainbow Warrior* was going to the United States in January. Would he manage her? It was an offer he couldn't refuse.

The *Warrior* crossed the North Atlantic in February 1981 to campaign against the slaughter of harp seals on the ice packs off the east coast of Canada. Crew members were arrested for dyeing seal pups' coats green to make them commercially worthless. A protest voyage was also made to Georges Bank, off the New England Coast, against oil and gas development in one of the world's richest fishing grounds.

Sawyer took over in March from Bruce Crammond, a New Zealand merchant seaman with Antarctic experience, who was in command briefly after Castle. But Crammond's Dutch girlfriend didn't like him going to sea all the time and she had sent a plane ticket to Boston with an ultimatum: join me now or never see me again. Crammond went.

'Bogey' Bouquet, a straightforward skipper who didn't like dealing with the press and public, returned for a brief spell to help Sawyer. American Peter Willcox, who had an unlimited master's ocean-going ticket, also joined the *Warrior*. Aged 28, Willcox had been sailing for the past couple of years on the square-rigged *Regina Maris*, a whale research vessel operated by the Ocean Research Foundation. Before that he had been skipper of the ecology boat *Clearwater*, a 30-metre Hudson River sloop.

The *Rainbow Warrior* was in a wretched state after the Spanish freedom dash. The propeller had been twisted in the Newfoundland ice, there were many leaks, electronics were poor and the wiring fouled. The propulsion system was in particularly bad shape. Some Greenpeace leaders just wanted to patch her up and dispatch her on a one-way protest to Moruroa in May. Sawyer had more faith.

After a generator caught fire, it was decided to change the whole propulsion system, switch the electrics from DC to AC current and give the ship a massive refit. One shipyard in Boston quoted $650,000 for the job and said it would take at least six months. Professional engineers said it wouldn't work.

Instead, the *Rainbow Warrior* was taken to Stonington, on Deer Island, Maine, to a cheap shipyard where Greenpeace volunteers were able to do most of the work. At the time a new Greenpeace ship had just been bought,

Left: The Rainbow Warrior *off the northern tip of Newfoundland in March 1981, caught in an ice pack during an anti-sealing campaign.* (Pierre Gleizes/Greenpeace)

the Amsterdam-registered pilot boat *Sirius*, and a telex message was sent to Sawyer saying that the 'R Dub' should be scrapped. It angered him but he ignored it.

A budget of $129,000 was set for the whole refit, including $83,000 for the new 600 hp General Motors Detroit diesel engine and $19,000 for two replacement generators.

It was an exhausting time. The volunteers worked from 7 a.m. to 9 p.m. Little food could be bought out of the budget; they were forced to raid lobster pots and junk yards to get by. Willcox spent days slicing off a lead-covered copper cable to sell for scrap and he was covered from head to toe in lead dust. Biologist Kevin Downing was suffering from a hernia but wouldn't undergo surgery. He clutched his abdomen with one hand while carrying things around with the other. Everybody was coated in grime and stank from diesel.

It took 11 weeks to finish the refit and the ship was 'reborn' in November 1981 while the *Vega* was on her third protest voyage to Moruroa. 'Bogey' had returned to Britain. Willcox, inspired to join Greenpeace by the book *Warriors of the Rainbow*, was now skipper and would be until she was bombed.

The following year the *Rainbow Warrior* launched successful campaigns against chemical waste dumping in the New York Bight, and against sealing in the Gulf of St Lawrence. It took the ship two weeks to battle through the ice pack to reach the hunt and crew members were again arrested for saving the lives of several hundred seal pups.

During the campaign the European Economic Community effectively ended the commercial sealing industry by banning imports of seal pup skins.

Six months after an anti-whaling campaign in Peru during which the Warrior was arrested for 'piracy', the Peruvian Government bowed out of whaling. In 1983 the *Warrior* campaigned against oil and gas development off the Californian coast and against United States Navy plans to dump ageing nuclear submarines at sea.

Now the *Rainbow Warrior* faced her most dramatic campaign so far — a cheeky visit to Siberia to document illegal Soviet whaling. The California gray whale breeds off Mexico and migrates to the Bering Sea. Protected by Mexico, Canada and the United States, the whales were being slaughtered once they reached Soviet waters. The Soviet Government claimed the whale hunt was being used to feed the Siberian *Inuit* (Eskimo) population.

After the short trip in July 1983 across the Bering Strait from Nome, Alaska, the *Warrior* sent three Zodiacs ashore at dawn near the whaling station of Lorino. Five of the crew went ashore to film evidence of whale meat being used for mink feed, and to pass out pamphlets in Russian among incredulous Inuit workers unloading a coal barge. A Soviet

Left: *When the* Rainbow Warrior *crew arrived in the Bering Sea on 22 July 1983 to recover the seven captives from the Soviet Union, a Russian crewman gave them a bottle of vodka as well.* (Richard Dawson/Greenpeace)

Army truck sped down the hill and a squad of teenage Russian soldiers arrested them at gunpoint.

Second mate Pat Herron drove an inflatable ashore in a bid to rescue the others. He was seized as well. Skipper Willcox, convinced he couldn't negotiate the release of his crewmates, left for Alaska. A military helicopter buzzed the *Rainbow Warrior* and a freighter tried to cut her off. Within an hour a Soviet warship was on her tail as well. Fearing capture, film of the arrests was loaded on to an inflatable with enough fuel for 12 hours and first mate Jim Henry volunteered for the risky dash to the Alaskan coast. But the helicopter forced Henry into the sea and dragged him out with a rope. Seven crew members were now in Soviet hands.

The *Warrior* recovered the spinning inflatable with its valuable film and eluded the pursuers.

'After a wild chase by the Russians, a ship belonging to Greenpeace is in safe harbour tonight,' said a CBS television news bulletin:

The *Rainbow Warrior* is back in American waters near Nome, Alaska, but seven of her anti-whaling protesters remain in custody in Siberia after being captured by the Russian military. The Greenpeace force had gone ashore to take pictures of a Soviet whaling station. They photographed a Russian whale-meat processing plant which they claim was outlawed by world whaling agreements.

The capture provoked a major diplomatic clash between Washington and Moscow. Five days later the arrested crew were freed — and handed over to the *Rainbow Warrior* in a mid-ocean rendezvous.

Heading for San Francisco Bay, Willcox surprised the crew. In a dummy run for the Pacific voyage he hoisted a spinnaker he had bought for $40, hitching it to the crow's nest and a cargo boom. When it was pulling well, he ordered the engine shut down. The trawler was *sailing* for the first time.

Footnotes to Chapter One

1 *Moru* and *roa* are Mangarevian dialect words together meaning 'a place of a great secret'. Moruroa was bastardised to Mururoa by French Navy cartographers. Tahitians and most Pacific publications use *Moruroa*.

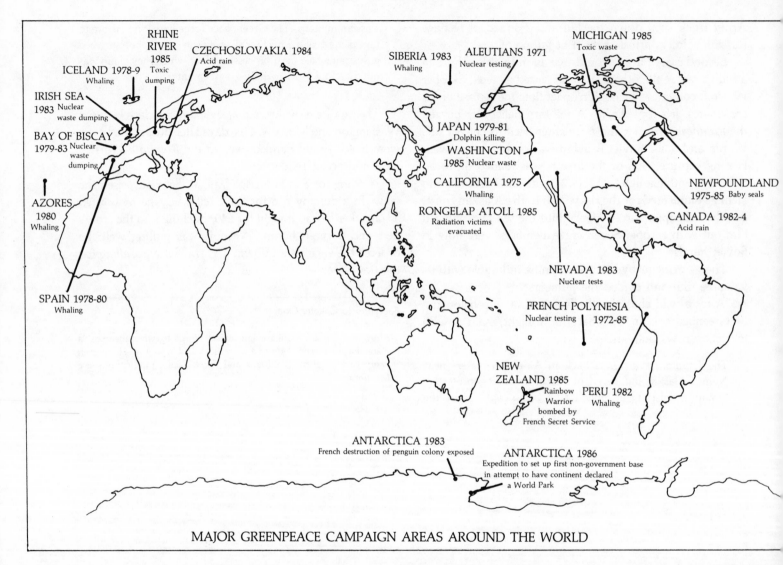

MICHIGAN 1985
Toxic waste

RHINE
RIVER
1985
Toxic
dumping

CZECHOSLOVAKIA 1984
Acid rain

SIBERIA 1983
Whaling

ALEUTIANS 1971
Nuclear testing

ICELAND 1978-9
Whaling

IRISH SEA
1983 Nuclear
waste dumping

BAY OF BISCAY
1979-83 Nuclear
waste
dumping

JAPAN 1979-81
Dolphin killing

WASHINGTON
1985 Nuclear waste

CALIFORNIA 1975
Whaling

NEWFOUNDLAND
1975-85 Baby seals

CANADA 1982-4
Acid rain

AZORES
1980
Whaling

RONGELAP ATOLL 1985
Radiation victims
evacuated

NEVADA 1983
Nuclear tests

SPAIN 1978-80
Whaling

FRENCH POLYNESIA
Nuclear testing   1972-85

NEW
ZEALAND 1985
Rainbow
Warrior
bombed by
French Secret Service

PERU 1982
Whaling

ANTARCTICA 1983
French destruction of penguin colony exposed

ANTARCTICA 1986
Expedition to set up first non-government base
in attempt to have continent declared
a World Park

MAJOR GREENPEACE CAMPAIGN AREAS AROUND THE WORLD

CHAPTER TWO

The curse called Bravo

In a sense the Marshall Islanders are the first victims of the Third World War. They are the first culture in the history of our race which has been effectively destroyed by radiation. — Australian filmmaker Dennis O'Rourke

JOHN ANJAIN will always remember 1 March 1954 as the day of the double sunrise. One sun rose from the east, as usual, and the other from the west. 'We heard a noise like thunder. We saw some strange clouds over the horizon. But the sun in the west faded away,' Anjain recalls.

He also remembers it as the day it 'snowed' on his coral atoll. 'In the afternoon something began falling from the sky upon our island. It looked like ash from a fire. It fell on me, it fell on my wife, it fell on our infant son. It fell on the trees, and on the roofs of our houses. It fell on the reef, and into the lagoon.

'We were very curious about this ash falling from the sky. Some people put it in their mouths and tasted it. One man rubbed it into his eye to see if it would cure an old ailment. People walked in it, and children played with it.'

At the time, Anjain, now 63, was mayor of Rongelap Atoll in the Ralik ('sunset') chain in what is now the republic of the Marshall Islands, part of the United States-administered Trust Territory of the Pacific Islands. The second sun he saw that day was the fireball from an American thermonuclear explosion codenamed Bravo. The snow was radioactive fallout.

Since then, the *baijin* (poison), as the islanders call it, has caused much illness and forced them to abandon their ancestral homeland and move to another island.

When the Americans exploded the H-bomb Bravo on Bikini Atoll, almost 6,500 kilometres north-west of New Zealand, it was the height of the Cold War. The bomb was a 15-megaton giant, more than 1,000 times as powerful as the bomb which devastated Hiroshima, and its explosion opened a terrifying new chapter in the arms race.

Hundreds of people living on the nearby downwind atolls of Rongelap, 150 kilometres to the east, and Rongerik and Utirik, were exposed to the massive fallout. Tonnes of pulverised coral and debris were sucked up into a fireball 40 kilometres above Bikini and dumped on other islands. On Rongelap, 64 people were contaminated, as were another 18 Rongelapese on nearby Ailingnae where they were cutting copra and catching fish. Also hit downwind by the fallout were 23 men on board the Japanese fishing trawler *Lucky Dragon* and 28 United States Air Force technicians who were monitoring Bravo from Rongerik Atoll.

At least five of the 66 nuclear tests at Bikini and Enewetak Atolls between 1946 and 1958 rained fallout on Rongelap Atoll.

'Later on, in the early evening it rained,' Anjain continued, sitting in the shade of a pandanus tree beside Rongelap lagoon. 'The rain fell on the roofs of our houses. It washed away the ash. The water mixed with the ash which fell into our water catchments. Men, women and children drank that water. It didn't taste like rainwater and it was dark yellow, sometimes black. But people drank it anyway.

'Then, the next day, some Americans came to our island. They had a machine [geiger counter] with them. They went around the island. They looked very worried and talked rapidly to each other. They told us we must not drink the water in our catchment tanks. They left — without explaining anything.

'By now most of the people were sick. Many vomited and felt weak. Later, the hair of men, women and children began to fall out. A lot of people had burns on their skin.

'On the third day some ships came. Americans again came on our island. They explained that we were in great danger because of the ash. They said, "If you don't leave, you will all die".'

The islanders were evacuated to Kwajalein Atoll, 160 kilometres south-east, for 'decontamination'. Three years later they were allowed to return to Rongelap, declared safe by American scientists in spite of 'slight lingering radiation'. No clean-up operation was carried out.

Bravo was exploded a week after Anjain's son, Lekoj, had his first birthday. Eighteen years later the boy died at the National Institute of Health clinic in Bethesda, Maryland, from acute myelogenous leukemia. His death was the first to be blamed on the fallout. Although the Atomic Energy Commission tried to keep the death quiet, American journalist Stewart Alsop shared a room with Lekoj and wrote a moving account of his struggle for life in *Newsweek*.

Two other of his sons, Zacharias, 38, and George, 35, have needed surgery, like Lekoj, for thyroid tumours.

Schoolteacher Billiet Edmond was also up at dawn on Bravo day. He was cleaning up around his home and shared coffee with Anjain. He later recorded his vivid impressions in a 30-page diary:

March 1, 1954: It was between five and six when the first flash came . . . from that overwhelming and most frightening event. I was completely oblivious of my surroundings and I couldn't even think to look at my watch.

The mayor also joined me and my family to observe that frightening but impressive episode . . . As the lightning faded, a huge and fiery sunlike object rose up in the western part of the lagoon.

It was a sun for it was round, but it was much bigger than our sun. It *was* a sun for it was lighting the sky and giving off heat . . . yet its intensity was far greater and

Above and left: John Anjain with a nephew. In Rongelap's cemetery is the grave of his son Lekoj, who died of myelogenous leukemia in 1972, aged 18. He had celebrated his first birthday just 10 days before the Bravo fallout. The plaque reads 'Lekoj Anjain: Born 21 February 1953, died 15 November 1972. Bethesda, Maryland USA.'

invincible, and it was much brighter, which left all of us aghast.

As the terrible fireball completely rose above the western horizon, its upper portion erupted and a combination of blended particles spurted out and upward, burning.

None of us could move, but everyone stared at the fireball without a word. In just one fraction of a second, the queer-looking fiery object became a giant mushroom, and then another one, and then another, and still another grew upon another . . . the whole atmosphere turned bloody coloured — and the *heat!*

The heat was threatening. It stung and burned our exposed skins. I could see some signs of movement as everyone withdrew from the terrible heat . . .

The explosion! Louder than any 100 of the strongest Second World War bombs bursting *together* . . . the ever-frightening sound accompanied by a tornado-powered wind sweeping through our land, twisting coconut trees, uprooting bushes, smashing windows, doors and overturning one house. My 10-year-old boy was knocked down . . . thatched roofs of most houses were blown out.

At 11.30, the classes were dismissed . . . the pupils and I were greeted by powderlike particles as they began to fall on the land . . . it didn't alarm the islanders whom I met on my way home. Even the children who were walking with me were playing with it. They ran through it, and they tried to catch it as if to see who could collect the most. . . .

As we approached the dim, foggy sunset . . . the ashes took effect on the islanders in a sudden and most crushing way. An unusually irritating itching punished the islanders . . . the kids were violently crying, scratching . . .

March 2, 1954: School was called off, and almost all our organised activities on the atoll came to a complete halt . . . By about 9 a.m. I had a funny feeling — nausea. It was mild, but steady and after a while all food and water I tried to consume was bitter.

My boy was even worse — he had vomited quite frequently . . . eventually *all* the islanders were affected. Some cases of diarrhoea developed with the young children and a few elders . . .

March 3, 1954: Early in the morning, an American destroyer made its way through the south pass into Rongelap's calm blue lagoon and headed toward the main village on the largest island.

Through an interpreter, we were told that we were moving from our home *immediately*. We were under orders not to take anything at all besides our bodies and our clothes.

Like a military invasion, the evacuation was conducted in a most dramatic and forceful fashion. We were in a complete state of shock.

Shortly after their evacuation to Kwajalein, most of the Rongelapese were suffering from burns on their ears, necks, feet, and their eyes were painful. Within weeks, many of them had lost their hair.

United States Government scientists calculated that each

Right: *United States military personnel use geiger counters to check evacuated Rongelap Islanders for radiation three days after the Bravo fallout in 1954.* (US Armed Forces)

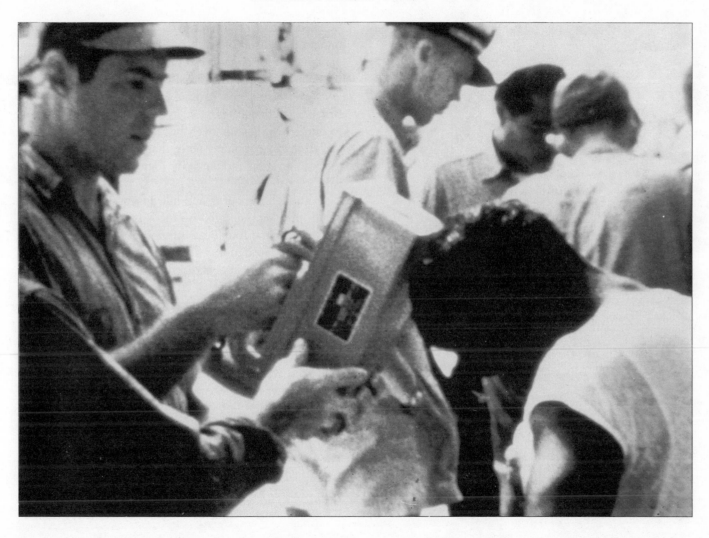

exposed islander had received a 'whole body external radiation dose' of 190 rads — 380 times the current legal *annual* limit for American residents. The exposed islanders on Ailingnae got an external dose of 110 rads.

Nevertheless, the Atomic Energy Commission called Bravo a 'routine atomic test' in a press statement designed to calm growing fears over the fallout. Of the Marshallese and Americans, it simply noted that they were 'unexpectedly exposed' to some radioactivity. 'There were no burns. All were reported well.'

Although the burns and hair loss were the immediate health problems suffered by the Rongelapese, worse was to come. In the four years after Bravo, exposed women from Rongelap had miscarriage and stillbirth rates more than double those of unexposed women. Seventy-seven per cent of those on Rongelap who were aged under 10 when exposed to the Bravo explosion have had surgery to remove thyroid tumours.

Lekoj Anjain's death was the first blamed on the fallout but there has been at least one other victim: a 64-year-old man who was exposed to high-dose radiation died from gastric cancer in 1974. And, according to noted American

Left: *In 1957, three years after the Bravo fallout, the Atomic Energy Commission declared Rongelap safe. But an official report said, 'Even though the radioactive contamination of Rongelap is considered perfectly safe for human habitation, the levels of activity are higher than those found in other inhabited locations in the world.'* (US Armed Forces)

SPECIAL EXAMINATION GROUP
RONGELAP EXPOSED

NAME Ellen Boas
SEX F   I.D. NO. 18
BIRTHDATE 1930
ISLAND OF BIRTH Rongelap
MARRIED yes   NO. OF CHILDREN 13

Above and right: *Ellen Boas was 24 when she was exposed to radioactive fallout from Bravo. She was taken to Kwajalein Atoll by a United States Navy destroyer. 'They made us throw away our clothes and they gave us bathing suits or underwear to put on — it was very embarrassing for us. When we left, our bodies were aching — my feet were burning and I couldn't walk without much pain.' Today she is reminded of the ordeal by the red 'Exposed' card she carries and the scar on her throat where a thyroid tumour was removed.*

researcher Dr John Gofman of the University of California, Berkeley, all Rongelapese aged under 15 when exposed to the Bravo fallout face a premature death from cancer. Scientists from the AEC, now the Department of Energy, began examining the islanders after they were moved to Kwajalein and have returned to Rongelap to do follow-up tests at least once a year since then, as part of an official study. They bring their own food from the United States and do not eat local coconut crabs, turtles, clams, coconuts and breadfruit.

A document from the Brookhaven National Laboratory in New York, produced three years after Bravo, said:

> Greater knowledge of [radiation] effects on human beings is badly needed . . . Even though the radioactive contamination of Rongelap Island is considered perfectly safe for human habitation, the levels of activity are higher than those found in other inhabited locations in the world. The habitation of these people on the island will afford the most valuable ecological radiation data on human beings.[1]

The Rongelapese have for years accused United States Government scientists of using them as guinea pigs. They claim that their exposure to Bravo was not an accident but part of an experiment to test the effects of radiation on human beings. The United States Government has consistently claimed that the fallout was 'accidental' and caused by an 'unpredicted shift in winds'. However, in 1984 a declassified Defense Nuclear Agency report surfaced confirming that the fallout was in fact *not* an accident. The report said that six hours before the blast, weather briefings showed winds at 20,000 feet were heading for Rongelap.

Four of the United States servicemen exposed on Rongerik and now suffering illnesses blamed on the fallout filed a civil lawsuit in 1982 against government agencies. They allege that the Government and contractors were negligent in carrying out the test and engaged in a 'conspiracy to cover up and conceal' vital scientific information.

'The wind had been blowing straight at us for days before the test,' one of the four veterans, Gene Curbow, told the *New York Times*. Curbow was a senior weather technician on Rongerik who took radio-sound weather measurements up to an altitude of 30,000 metres before and after Bravo. 'It was blowing straight at us during the test, and straight at us after it. The wind never shifted.'

Curbow, 52, and the other veterans claimed they suffered from a variety of illnesses including painful skin rashes and cancer, tumours, heart and thyroid conditions, and urinary and bladder disorders that they said were related to Bravo. Three of them said they had difficulty fathering children or had had sickly offspring.

Senator Jeton Anjain, Rongelap's representative in the Marshall Islands *Nitijela*, or parliament, a younger brother of John Anjain, said: 'That this massive hydrogen bomb went ahead in spite of this information demonstrates that the nuclear experiments — and not the welfare of the people — were the United States Government's priority.'

During 1985 Dennis O'Rourke, one of Australia's leading documentary filmmakers, released *Half Life* — the title being a cruel double play on the unit used to measure the decay of radioactivity and the fate of the Rongelapese. He spent two years in the Marshall Islands and the United States, where he obtained documents and film footage which leave the official American version of events even more shaky. The film was made with the support of the BBC and is expected to be screened on the American non-commercial network PBS.

O'Rourke, a former ABC assistant cameraman who won a string of awards for his documentary *Yumi Yet* about the independence of Papua New Guinea, never believed when he started his research that the Americans set out deliberately to expose the Rongelapese to radiation.

'But at the end of the project,' he later admitted to the *National Times*, 'I can say that they certainly allowed the exposure to happen, and have used the victims ever since as guinea pigs to study the long-term effects of radiation on human beings who have to live in a contaminated environment. This will be all of us in the event of nuclear war.'

Among the many questionable decisions made by the Brookhaven scientists was allowing the Rongelapese to return to their atoll three years after Bravo. Eager to get on with the radiation studies, the scientists allowed the exposed islanders, and those who had not been on Rongelap when the fallout dusted the atoll, to return in July 1957.

After only a year back on the atoll, scientists reported the Rongelapese body levels of radioactive zinc[65], strontium[90] and caesium[137] had risen rapidly. In 1966 Brookhaven scientists themselves ate pandanus and coconuts from Rongelap under laboratory conditions. They reported their intake of strontium[90] over a week was 20 times higher than normal. Yet the islanders were still told their atoll was safe to live on.

Five years later, a Japanese medical research team issued a report critical of Brookhaven for allowing the people to go home: 'It was a great mistake to permit the people of Rongelap to return . . . without sufficient work having been done to remove radioactive pollution from the islands.' It added that the islanders who had not originally been exposed to Bravo absorbed a considerable dose of radioactive nucleides from the environment. Consequently the 'unexposed' group actually became an 'exposed' group.

In 1978, more than two decades after Rongelap was declared safe, the Department of Energy completed an aerial radiation survey of the northern Marshalls, including Rongelap and Bikini Atolls. The survey found that several of the northern islands of Rongelap were more heavily contaminated than parts of Bikini. Early the next year, scientists went to Rongelap and told the people the northern islands — vital for food gathering and copra production — were too radioactive to visit.

Scientists of the Department of Energy check only the 59 people originally exposed on Rongelap who are still living, while using the small 'unexposed' group for a control population. The department doesn't systematically follow up the entire population of more than 500, including Rongelapese now living on other atolls. Exposed islanders carry red identity cards and the unexposed group, green.

'The Department of Energy's checks are the ultimate in degradation for these people — it is like animals being loaded onto an experimental conveyor while the scientists maintain an arrogant silence,' said Glenn Alcalay, a Marshallese-speaking anthropologist. 'When one considers the international fuss being made over the search for Nazi war criminal Dr Jose Mengele, it is sobering to remember there are any number of Dr Mengeles being given free rein in the Marshall Islands.'

Alcalay, 35, a consultant with the Washington-based National Committee for Radiation Victims, was a Peace Corps volunteer on Utirik Atoll between 1975 and 1977 when he helped initiate legal and legislative proceedings which led to some congressional compensation for the people of Bikini, Eniwetak, Rongelap and Utirik. Congressional compensation had begun in 1964 when $11,000 was paid to each of the exposed people on Rongelap. In 1977 Congress voted a further payment of about $1 million to both Rongelap and Utirik. Anybody having thyroid surgery was paid $25,000 and the survivors of a person dying from a radiation-linked malignancy such as leukemia were entitled to $100,000. At present, claims totalling more than $US5,000 million have been filed by more than 3,000 Marshallese, including many Rongelap Islanders, in damages lawsuits against the United States Government. But their chances hinge on whether a Compact of Free Association, which passed through Congress early in 1986, will uphold the islanders' rights to sue.

A report, prepared for the litigants by American researcher Dr Thomas Hamilton, found there was ample data to show people living on Rongelap during the last 30 years had significant levels of radiation exposure from land and food-chain contamination. This applied also to the control population. He said:

> The high-dose exposed Rongelapese are possibly the most irradiated group of people on earth. A critical question is, therefore, whether they are developing increasing risk while living on their atoll of Rongelap . . . It may be necessary for the Rongelap people to relocate.

Professor Karl Morgan, former director of health physics at Oak Ridge National Laboratory, has thoroughly examined all the United States Government studies conducted by Lawrence Livermore Laboratory and Brookhaven. He considers the conclusions in these studies underestimate the health risks of radiation by a factor of between 10 and 100, and in some cases by a factor of 1,000. The discrepancy resulted from the presence of 'hot spots' as well as individuals being at higher risk because of age, health and other factors.

Right: *A Rongelap couple believed to have been prematurely aged by radiation.*

When the Rongelapese were told the radiation levels on some of their atoll's islands were higher than at Bikini, their fears grew. One half of their atoll, including their choicest food-gathering area, had been put off-limits.

'While we might understand the quarantine,' said Senator Anjain, 'I'm afraid the lagoon fish, sea turtles and coconut crabs in our diet don't understand it as they move around freely and end up in our dinner!'

The islanders began to realise they would have to leave their atoll if their children and grandchildren were to have a chance. They sought help from the *Nitijela*. However, while they won a unanimous parliamentary vote of approval in August 1983 for their move, they failed to get any financial or logistical help. The reason was partly internal politics — Senator Anjain had earlier resigned as Health Minister and joined the Opposition parliamentary bloc — and partly because the Government didn't want to upset Washington when a huge aid package was at stake during negotiations over the Compact.

No help came from the United States Government either, probably to avoid any acknowledgement of the problem it had created. However, a belated congressional vote pledged $500,000 for an independent radiological survey, long sought by the islanders and expected to be conducted by West Germany's University of Bremen, and $3.2 million for resettlement. But the latter amount depends on the survey confirming the risks.

Determined to move, Senator Anjain appealed late in 1984 to Greenpeace, which was already planning a visit to the Marshall Islands by the *Rainbow Warrior* the following year.

Greenpeace agreed. Within six months the *Warrior* would be at Rongelap.

Footnote to Chapter Two

1. Robert A. Conard, *March 1957 Medical Survey of Rongelap and Utirik People*, Brookhaven National Laboratory, June 1958.

CHAPTER THREE

From Jacksonville to Majuro

Greenpeace has had a lot of visions. Fitting the trawler
Rainbow Warrior *with sails for the Pacific was one of*
them.

— Greenpeace *Examiner*

DUTCHMAN HENK Haazen and New Zealander Bunny McDiarmid first saw the *Rainbow Warrior* in a slipyard in the dock wasteland of Jacksonville, Florida, during the autumn of 1984. She was neglected. Insects and rats had moved on board. She looked lifeless.

She had been taken to Jacksonville, Florida, for an ambitious refit costing at least $US110,000. It had been decided to add sails to help equip the ship for a year-long Pacific peace voyage. It would halve the fuel bill for the 30,000-kilometre expedition to the Marshall Islands, Kiribati, Vanuatu, New Zealand and Moruroa Atoll.

Ed Simmons, an American electrical engineer who had helped install the ship's 600-horsepower diesel engine and new generators three years earlier, had been entrusted with the job of directing the sail-power metamorphosis for the *Warrior*. But it was too much for him and he was replaced by Athel von Koettlitz.

In spite of the state of the *Rainbow Warrior*, Haazen and McDiarmid were inspired. They had come to Jacksonville in the veteran peace ship *Fri* and with them was crewmate Alice Heather. She had seen the *Warrior* earlier, when the ship was in Falmouth, England, and knew her way around it. So she took them on board for a tour.

Haazen, a 31-year-old, tall, strong engineer with his fair hair drawn back in a ponytail, and energetic, freckle-faced McDiarmid, a 28-year-old sociology graduate from Canterbury University, who had left New Zealand almost seven years before and never been back, liked the idea of the peace voyage. They hadn't worked with Greenpeace before, but they had a lot of sailing experience. Recently they had returned from a trip on the *Fri* to Nicaragua where they had delivered medical supplies. The fledgling Sandinista republic's struggle against American attempts to sap its lifeblood had created a deep impression.

Haazen and McDiarmid believed the journey to Rongelap was an important mission. They sent an application letter which was backed up by another *Fri* veteran, Martini Gotje, 36, by then first mate on the *Warrior*. Within a couple of weeks they got a phone call from Greenpeace's marine division in the East London docks. Yes, they were

accepted — Haazen as third engineer and McDiarmid as a deckhand.

The Pacific voyage was also beginning to take detailed shape for Steve Sawyer, now one of Greenpeace's five international directors and the man co-ordinating the campaign. Greenpeace had been planning a major expedition into the Pacific with the *Rainbow Warrior* for four years. Elaine Shaw, of the Greenpeace New Zealand office in Auckland, who has close links with the grassroots Nuclear-Free and Independent Pacific Movement, had been pushing for such a mission even longer. But it had always been put off. More urgent protests against nuclear waste dumping in European waters and anti-whaling campaigns, and lack of finance for the sail conversion, got in the way.

There had already been four protests to Moruroa, several of them spectacular, by the veteran 12-metre yacht *Vega* (*Greenpeace III*). But it hadn't been a campaign priority since 1975 when French nuclear tests were forced underground and when David McTaggart, now chairman of Greenpeace International, won a victory in the French courts. A tribunal ruled then that a French Navy minesweeper had rammed *Vega* at Moruroa in 1972. The court ordered the navy to pay damages. However, in the second part of McTaggart's lawsuit — an accusation of armed piracy, documented by photographs — the court declared it was 'not competent to judge'. Even though it was only

Left: *The* Rainbow Warrior *under sail on her Pacific peace voyage.*

half a victory, it was still a blow to the French nuclear testing programme. The *Vega* followed with protests to Moruroa in 1981 and 1982 but they did not receive as much publicity, in spite of the *Vega* being temporarily seized.

And now a new issue was challenging Moruroa as a *cause célèbre* in the Pacific, or rather a reawakening of a little-known issue — Rongelap and the health legacy from American nuclear tests in the Marshall Islands.

The problems of the Pacific were new for Sawyer. But he was quick to learn. Early in 1983 he met NFIP activists including Bernie Keldermans of Belau, Rongelap islander Julian Riklon, and American journalist Giff Johnson in Boston. Sawyer had come off the *Warrior* about three months before and was working at the Boston office. He was also Greenpeace's United States representative on the international Greenpeace Council.

In February 1984 a proposal was put together for a Pacific campaign that year. But it wasn't well prepared and had to be postponed when seven *Rainbow Warrior* crew members were arrested during an attempt to document illegal Soviet whaling operations based at Lorino, Siberia.

At the time there was also a lot of internal wrangling within Greenpeace about whether to send the Amsterdam-registered sister ship *Sirius* into the Arabian Gulf. Iran and Iraq were at war and vast amounts of crude oil were being spewed into the Gulf at Kharg island after the Iraqis had bombed Iranian oilfields and refineries.

The war was preventing capping of the wells. Several Greenpeace leaders favoured sending 'a little green boat with rainbows on it' to break the political stalemate so the wells could be plugged. Greenpeace was in close touch with oil business professionals who would do the job.

But the deadlock continued. Although many Greenpeace people supported the idea, others thought it was too big and too risky. In the end it was shelved.

In June 1984 the Australian, New Zealand, Canadian and United States branches of Greenpeace held their first regional meeting in Hawaii where Sawyer met Elaine Shaw for the first time. He already knew Carol Stewart, another stalwart of the Auckland office. They began to draft an 'intelligent itinerary' for the *Rainbow Warrior* voyage to the Pacific in 1985. It was decided to address both the American and French nuclearisation of the Pacific, and to tie in the health problems of 'atomic' veterans as well. (The atomic veterans are the approximately 250,000 former US servicemen who were exposed to radioactive fallout from the atmospheric nuclear testing programme, 1945–62.)

The plan would also focus world attention on President Reagan's strategic defence initiative, or Star Wars, research at Kwajalein Atoll and on the Marshallese victims of radiation, such as the Rongelapese. In the middle leg of the voyage, the *Rainbow Warrior* would give support to Kiribati and Nauru's attempts through the London Dumping Convention to outlaw nuclear-waste dumping at sea. The ship would then visit Vanuatu, a staunch anti-nuclear nation, in an effort to persuade the Government to join the LDC and back Kiribati's initiative, something it curiously had not done so far.

Talking about the Marshall Islands, the first name that came to everybody's lips was Giff Johnson. Sawyer had hoped at one stage to hire him as Greenpeace's co-ordinating expert in the Central Pacific. Johnson, now editor of the *Marshall Islands Journal*, the republic's only newspaper, was then with the Hawaii-based Pacific Concerns Research Centre spawned by the NFIP movement. But he was already planning on moving to Majuro with his Marshallese wife, health specialist Darlene Keju.

Sawyer phoned Johnson to set up a meeting in mid-October. Johnson was working full time on his book *Collision Course at Kwajalein*, an account of the nuclear exploitation of Micronesia by the United States. They met in Seattle because they had mutual friends there.

One thing they quickly agreed on: Greenpeace couldn't go barging into Kwajalein in their typical, high-profile, direct-action style. It wouldn't make sense to the islanders and the campaign probably wouldn't succeed unless Greenpeace had the support of the local people.

On the last day of their three-day meeting, they started discussing specific possibilities and relating them to the Rongelap tragedy. What Sawyer didn't know at the time was that Johnson had just got an angry letter from Senator Jeton Anjain. The senator had just received a list of the PCRC priorities for 1985 and Rongelap was not even mentioned.

They discussed Rongelap. They thought that as an introduction to the Marshalls some kind of symbolic evacuation would be good.

Perhaps some people from Rongelap, or another atoll contaminated by fallout, could be taken on board the *Rainbow Warrior* to look around for a place to resettle?

They decided to try out the idea on Senator Anjain. Johnson flew back to Honolulu while Sawyer returned to Washington. About three days later, Johnson was on the phone: 'Hey, I was speaking to Jeton and he was leaping up and down, all excited about it.'

Anjain boarded a plane for Honolulu almost immediately. The three of them discussed the plan over the phone, Anjain and Johnson in Honolulu, and Sawyer in Washington.

Sawyer got a misleading image of Anjain from the phone. The senator appeared such a quiet, soft-spoken person that Sawyer gained an initial impression of him as a much younger man, not a 53-year-old former cabinet minister. Certainly he didn't picture him as the 'hard-core' leader of the Rongelapese. Sawyer had been unprepared for the mild-mannered Marshallese, a people who don't even have a word for *enemy* in their language.

'To hell with this symbolic business — we want to move,' Anjain said. 'I have to move my people and if you can help us, please!'

'Well,' Sawyer replied, 'it sounds like what you want is a lot better than what we're talking about.'

The message was pretty clear: Greenpeace had the

Right: *The Pacific 'peace voyage' of the* Rainbow Warrior.

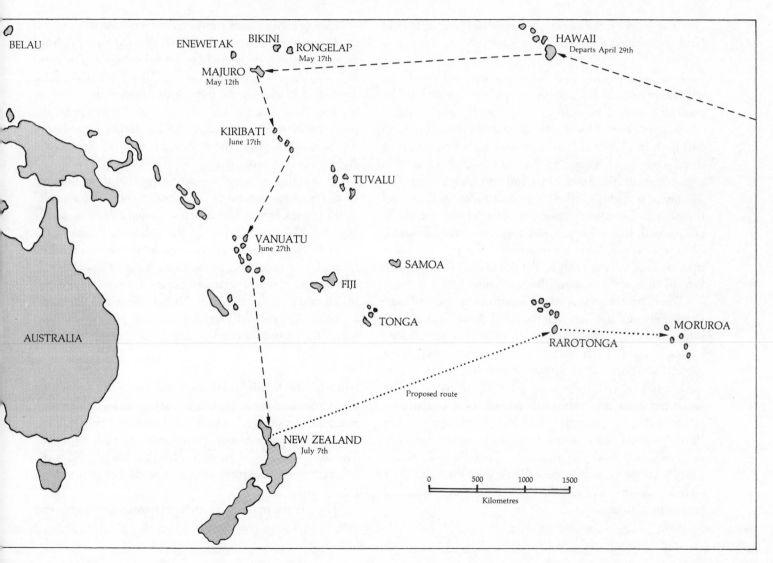

BELAU

ENEWETAK

BIKINI

RONGELAP
May 17th

MAJURO
May 12th

HAWAII
Departs April 29th

KIRIBATI
June 17th

TUVALU

VANUATU
June 27th

SAMOA

FIJI

TONGA

RAROTONGA

MORUROA

AUSTRALIA

Proposed route

NEW ZEALAND
July 7th

0   500   1000   1500

Kilometres

Rainbow Warrior; the Rongelapese wanted to move. Would Greenpeace help them shift immediately?

Back in Jacksonville, things were moving. But slowly. A few more people had arrived yet there seemed to be confusion over how to fit a trawler with a sailing rig.

Skipper Peter Willcox, the 32-year-old American who had been in charge of the *Rainbow Warrior* for the past three years, was on hand by the end of October. So were two friends of his, Sarah Underhill and David Rohl. Ula Thomsen, a highly skilled 24-year-old Danish fitter and turner who had been working at her trade for six years, got on with the welding. Chief engineer Davey Edward, 32, a laconic Yorkshireman with experience as a merchant-man on flag carriers such as the Blue Line and on North Sea oil rigs, arrived about the same time.

The *Warrior* was slipped at Marvin's Boatyard and Lane Crane Services, not far from the Pearl Bridge spanning St John's River. It seemed as if the trawler was surrounded by tug boats — even though there were probably never more than four — and a rusty scrapmetal dump.

Depressing. And the crew grew to intensely dislike Jacksonville. A tiny cubbyhole passed for a Greenpeace office in the city, and they had little local support. The Pacific seemed like a faraway dream as winter came.

Everybody worked long hours, dawn to dusk, sometimes six or seven days a week. They were tired and there were few diversions. Just a dingy bar nearby and occasional forays to a cinema.

One evening about eight of the crew and workers on the *Warrior* ended up in a real hillbilly nightspot. A huge taco bottle stood in the middle of the dancefloor. The band was playing country and western. All the bouncers were dressed in black — and they were bored stiff.

The *Warrior* crew got strange looks from the locals, partly because of their slightly shabby clothes. David Rohl was wearing a tank top, having dragged off a pullover. A bouncer sauntered over.

'Hey man, yer not allowed to wear that thing in here,' he said, leaning menacingly over the carpenter. 'Take 'er off.'

Rohl took him at his word and pulled off the tank top, exposing his chest, to put on the pullover. It was hot.

A couple of bouncers pounced on him and wrenched his neck in a headlock. In moments it was a brawl. Rohl, Martini Gotje and Hanne Sorensen were arrested and tossed into a cell for the night. Neither Gotje nor Sorensen, a slender 25-year-old Danish fitter and turner who had joined the crew as second engineer, had been involved in the incident.

Already, the *Rainbow Warrior* was becoming something of an anomaly in the annals of maritime design. Though many sailing ships have been dismasted and converted to power, few motor vessels have been refitted with masts. The rig design was done partly by Windship, a Norwell, Massachusetts, company with a good deal of improvising by the crew.

The day the masts, a 33-metre mainmast and a 26-metre

mizzen, were stepped was a big psychological boost. They had arrived at the shipyard a few weeks before, after their manufacture had dragged on and on. But they were delivered as bare steel pipes, nine centimetres thick. Track and fittings needed to be welded on and the deck prepared to support them. Twenty-four tonnes of ballast were added to the bilge to counterbalance the wind, and supports for the masts were built deep into the ship's keel.

To install the mizzen, the skylight above the mess room was ripped out and covered with a solid piece of steel, in turn lined with timber decking. A boomkin was welded to the stern to support mizzen stays. And to make room to set the sails, two metres were sawn off from each side of the wheelhouse and replaced with two platforms.

Finally the masts went up one Saturday afternoon, late in December. The crew carried out a ritual, burning some sprigs of rosemary and laying some coins where the masts were being stepped.

There was a big crowd. The crane drivers were nonchalant about the whole affair. They just picked up the mainmast, drove it back, hooked it in and there it was!

That night, the crew had a riotous party on board. In typical Greenpeace fashion, the best way to release the tension of the past couple of months was for everybody to get drunk.

The galley porthole looked out on to a concrete platform with a fridge blocking the view, or at least what passed for a view across the drab shipyard. The fridge had been a nuisance for weeks.

'I really *hate* fridges . . . and this one I just can't stand,' McDiarmid complained to Greenpeace technical director Athel von Koettlitz.

Von Koettlitz took the hint. Amid the revelry, he stepped ashore and gave the fridge a great shove. Down it crashed and they could finally see out of the galley.

Still a lot of work needed to be done. Rigging, booms, figuring out where to put things, winches, winchpads and pedestals. There was no master design for the boom goosenecks and the welders got carried away, creating an ungainly cumbersome structure. McDiarmid, eager to do some welding, took night school classes and got a chance to help. But Thomsen did most of the major welding tasks, except a bowsprit platform for the jib.

Ulf-Carston Schrooter, a German who had sailed on the *Clearwater*, and friend Melissa Ortquist from upstate New York, dropped in as volunteers for five days — and stayed for five weeks. Schrooter hadn't done much carpentry before, but he made a fine job of wood panelling in the wheelhouse and the mess.

Marine biologist Kevin Downing also gave a hand. When he was bosun on the *Sirius* he crewed with people who had sailed on the *Fri*. He reckoned they were so attuned to the spirit of the oceans that they often predicted whale sightings by their dreams.

All 11 crew were together by the time the *Warrior* was off the slip in mid-December. American radio operator Lloyd Anderson, at 41, the eldest, was last to arrive. Nathalie Mestre, a 20-year-old Swiss vegetarian cook, who

was the youngest, had turned up with Irish deckhand Grace O'Sullivan, 23. They shared the best cabin on board, under the wheelhouse, with no fewer than three portholes.

Born in the little village of Saignelegier, near Neuchâtel, in the foothills of the Jura mountains which cleave northwestern Switzerland from France, Mestre could speak fluent English, French, German and Spanish.

Rounding off the crew were the ship's doctor and deckhand Andy Biedermann, 29, also from Switzerland, and West German second mate Bene Hoffmann, 33, whose flowing beard and stature evoked an image of a Viking.

Willcox was clearly in charge, but with an air of we're-all-in-this-together. When it was time to install the new Japanese-designed colour radar screen in the wheelhouse, he considered each crewmember's opinion before deciding on its angle and height. Already the crew was revealing signs of the comradeship which would develop over the months ahead.

Sawyer flew to Majuro, capital of the Marshall Islands with a population of 12,000, in the second week of January 1985.

Left: *The crew, clockwise from top centre: radio operator Lloyd Anderson (in headband and glasses — US), engineer Henk Haazen (Holland), deckhand Bunny McDiarmid (NZ), captain Peter Willcox (US), mate Martini Gotje (Holland), deckhand Grace O'Sullivan (Ireland), mate Bene Hoffmann (W. Germany), engineer Davey Edward (Britain), cook Nathalie Mestre (left, Switzerland), engineer Hanne Sorensen (Denmark), deckhand and doctor Andy Biedermann (Switzerland). Fernando Pereira joined the* Warrior *in Hawaii.*

He wanted to meet Giff Johnson and Senator Anjain to work out details of the Rongelap evacuation. He was originally going to visit Rongelap as well to meet the islanders and to look at Mejato, a small island on the northwestern rim of Kwajalein Atoll. Although the Rongelapese had not yet made a decision on where to go, uninhabited Mejato had been offered and seemed the most suitable.

He had spent some time with Glenn Alcalay, a radiation victims researcher whom he already knew, and Australian filmmaker Dennis O'Rourke. But they, among others, were at first extraordinarily sceptical about the evacuation idea.

When Sawyer arrived in Majuro AMI, Airline of the Marshall Islands, wasn't flying. Its two Nomads were grounded, as they are for a lot of the time, so he couldn't go to Rongelap.

Instead, he went to Kwajalein, where he met about 100 Rongelapese who had taken refuge on Ebeye, a tiny dormitory island for the United States-run Kwajalein Missile Range. Among them were Lijon Eknilang, a miscarriage-plagued woman who had given testimony to the United Nations Trusteeship Council earlier in the year, and a former mayor, Nelson Anjain. Both shared their fears for the future of their people. Later, he checked with Majuro hospital to ask about medical supply needs.

After returning to Honolulu, Sawyer realised the evacuation was going to be the most important task of the voyage. Any publicity Greenpeace would get out of Kwajalein would be pure luck, unless the Americans tested a missile while the *Rainbow Warrior* was actually there.

The sails arrived on schedule in January, with the blocks, rigging and ropes. Willcox, Gotje and Hoffmann did the splicing. Railings and some of the leftover steelwork were also completed. Then the *Warrior* moved 30 kilometres downriver to Jacksonville's real harbour, Mayport. Across the St John's River, on the southern bank, was a big navy dockyard.

One day in February, the ship went for her maiden sail off the Florida coast. Amazing! Blaring out from the messroom was a dated Moody Blues tape called *On the Threshold of a Dream* as she clipped along at five knots.

Two weeks of sea trials went smoothly. Everything seemed to be working well; few adjustments were needed. On a fine day in a light wind, the *Warrior* would do about four knots. But blowing well, she could plough through the water at nine or 10 knots.

Now the *Rainbow Warrior* was almost ready to leave and she was under pressure to catch up on her campaign schedule. Thomsen and Schrooter were asked to go along as far as Hawaii. A few steelwork jobs and painting were still to be done. They left Mayport on 15 March — smack into a gale!

Three days out from Florida, radio antenna insulators on two backstays for the mainmast began to disintegrate and pieces of the insulators peppered the deck. The mast was jury-rigged with lines and block and tackle. But returning to Mayport was out of the question. Bad for morale.

Instead, the *Warrior* headed for the Bahamas. Within a week the ship was moored in Nassau harbour, surrounded by cruise liners. As the crew got on with repairs, somebody hit on the idea of setting up a dockside stall. With about 800 tourists passing a day, the crew began selling buttons, posters and 'Warriors of the Rainbow' T-shirts emblazoned with an Indian chief's head, a flower and the slogan:

When the earth is sick, the animals will begin to disappear. When that happens the warriors of the rainbow will come to save them.

They only made about $50 a day, but it helped to pay the mooring fee.

From Nassau to Panama, the crew had the best sailing on the entire voyage — a week at eight or nine knots a day. And there were no shipboard chores other than sailing watches.

Hardly anything happened on the next leg, a two-week dawdle to Hawaii. But now it was back to work again. The Pacific was so calm it was like being in dock. The *Warrior* steamed along day after day. There was no other choice, with the trade winds barely whispering.

Still the *Warrior* became fairly shipshape. The bulwarks were painted, the engineroom scrubbed and painted. And the wheelhouse was polished up and varnished. McDiarmid began sewing sail covers.

The English are a weird lot. Before the *Rainbow Warrior* reached Hawaii, a flying fish soared through Edward's porthole and flopped on the floor in the middle of the night.

A guided missile from Neptune. Edward couldn't believe his eyes — and nobody else believed him either.

'Well, I mean a bloody flying fish in your sleep!' Edward snorted. They thought I was dreaming. But then one landed in Ula Thomsen's cabin, too. And I said, "Thanks Ula!"'

'But think of the flying fish from their point of view,' added McDiarmid. 'Like there they are with wings flapping and suddenly they're in somebody's bunk.' Everybody laughed.

When the *Rainbow Warrior* rounded Diamond Head and reached Honolulu, Portuguese-born photographer Fernando Pereira was there to meet her in a chartered boat so he could photograph the ship under sail. Also waiting were Senator Jeton Anjain and an anxious-looking Steve Sawyer, wearing a Marshallese hat with the slogan: 'Ebeye Ocean Side'.

Three Rongelap islanders also joined the *Warrior* for the voyage to the Marshall Islands: *iroij* (chief) Kotak Loeak; Julian Riklon, treasurer of the Kwajalein Atoll Corporation, a landowners rights group; and another man from his office, Jolbo Samuel. I was the first of the journalists to go on board; the others joined the *Warrior* in Majuro.

After a dockside press conference, the *Rainbow Warrior* left for the Marshall Islands on the evening of 29 April. Reporter Catherine Enomoto, while writing about the

Right: *The three Marshall Islanders who joined the* Warrior *in Hawaii:* iroij *Kotak Loeak (left), Jolbo Samuel (crouched) and Julian Riklon.*

Rongelap evacuation mission in the next morning's *Star-Bulletin*, didn't want readers to confuse the ship's name with a local football team: 'The name comes from a Cree Indian tale, not the University of Hawaii mascot'.

Having the Rongelapese on board was a good cultural bridge for the crew, none of whom apart from Gotje on the *Fri* had had any contact with Pacific Islanders before. Chief Loeak, and Riklon, in particular, were able to brief the crew firsthand about the illnesses ravaging their people.

'Ever since the Bravo shot,' said Loeak, 'my people have lived in fear because of the many health problems we continue to face.'

Everybody got on well but a couple of things surprised Loeak. One was the largely beans-and-lentils vegetarian cuisine on board, which badly suited the Micronesian palate and was to eventually annoy some of the crew as well. The other was having five women among the crew — who were also frequently bare-breasted. In Marshallese custom, women don't do 'men's' work.

The *Rainbow Warrior* was welcomed at Majuro on 12 May in the wake of news of two fresh nuclear tests by France at Moruroa, including an unusually large 150-kiloton blast.

'Bastards,' raged Gotje. The crew telexed an angry message next day to French President Francois Mitterrand at the Elysée Palace:

We wish to express our outrage over these tests, not only for what they represent in terms of the nuclear weapons race, but also because of France's callous disregard for the wish of Pacific peoples everywhere to make their ocean a nuclear-free zone.

We are now engaged in an evacuation of the people of Rongelap Atoll . . . [who] were heavily contaminated by American nuclear tests in the 1940s and 1950s — and their islands remain dangerously radioactive to this day.

Must France continually repeat the mistakes of the United States and Britain in the Pacific? Must France continue to pompously ignore the tide of public opinion regionally and around the world which says, 'enough'?

The telex also warned Mitterrand the *Warrior* was heading for Moruroa later in the year, along with a peace flotilla from New Zealand. It appealed to his 'humanity' to end nuclear testing before it was too late.

Before leaving Majuro the crew had an open day on board the *Rainbow Warrior*. 'Drop in,' invited the local radio station. And the Marshallese did — in their hundreds. The old fish hold, converted into a video room containing a library of environmental and educational tapes, with titles like *The Nuclear Lagoon* and *Commandos of Conservation*, was the most popular corner of the ship. Majuro seemed flooded with schoolchildren wearing 'Save Our Seas' T-shirts dished out by the crew.

Even Foreign Minister Tony deBrum dropped in for a chat. DeBrum is probably one of the world's few foreign ministers who owns a bar, Charlie's Tavern. I cornered him for an interview in his office, in ex-wartime government buildings next to Majuro's former airfield. He denied the evacuation would reflect badly on the Marshall Islands Government.

'No, it's not an embarrassment at all. The Government has indicated its support for the evacuation by a unanimous resolution of the *Nitijela*,' said deBrum, a refreshingly candid man in a cabinet notorious for its silence towards foreign news media.' The involvement of Greenpeace means an opportunity for some international scrutiny of a problem that has plagued us for a long time — one that the United States refuses to acknowledge or recognise.

'The people don't want to live on a contaminated atoll and there is an alternative home for the time being. Also, the United States is quite willing to help out in other contaminated areas with much more sexy appeal — internationally — like Bikini and Enewetak, but not in the case of the people who were actually exposed to radiation.'

The *Marshall Islands Journal* and Guam's *Pacific Daily News* had front-page reports about how the Rongelap people were abandoning their ancestral home, and the arrival of the *Rainbow Warrior* to help them shift. One *Journal* story quoted American officials suddenly trying to pooh-pooh the fears of radiation.

'We see no radiological or medical reason to move,' said Andy Wilson, an American official who had been involved in a replanting project on Enewetak. Only a few weeks

Right: *Senator Jeton Anjain, the Rongelap Islanders' parliamentary representative, with Steve Sawyer. Their cooperation and friendship smoothed the way for Operation Exodus.*

previously he had admitted that coconuts grown on that atoll's northern islands were too radioactive to eat.

'Greenpeace and New Zealand are doing good things — standing up to the Americans,' said a feisty Majuro shopkeeper. 'We want to be nuclear free.'

Majuro gave a picture postcard view of a Pacific atoll. But outside the post office was a small notice which showed a more serious side.

'Listen to your bodies,' said the poster, which listed the signs of cancer.

CHAPTER FOUR

Operation Exodus

When we decided to leave Rongelap Atoll, the old people
cried to leave their homeland. But I said, 'What about
your grandchildren? Do you want them to die ?'
— Senator Jeton Anjain

A DAY after leaving Majuro — 16 May — the *Rainbow Warrior* passed close to the twin islands of Roi-Namur on the north-eastern tip of Kwajalein Atoll. Joined together by a coral-filled airstrip two decades ago, the islands now bristle with a forest of antennae and radar domes. Dwarfing the coconut palms is the giant Altair radar, used for ballistic missile research since 1970 and now the cornerstone of the United States Air Force's 'Pacific barrier' anti-satellite detection system. The network has two other monitoring stations — at San Miguel in the Philippines, and Guam.

The Altair at Roi-Namur is the most powerful of the three radars. It is capable of detecting and tracking objects at an altitude of 40,000 kilometres, higher than the orbits of many spacecraft. It is one of only two air force radars capable of high-altitude tracking.

As the *Rainbow Warrior* passed, the big dish swung on its axis, seemingly pointing in our direction.

'The bastards are nervous,' chuckled first mate Martini Gotje.

'The microwave emissions from the Altair are dangerous,' cautioned Sawyer. 'It makes any protest risky if you're close by in front of it. A couple of years ago a maintenance guy on Roi-Namur gotten caught like that. He gotten fried — lost his eyes!'

We now had 25 people on board. Besides the crew of 11, and Sawyer, Anjain, and Julian Riklon, there were four other islanders: Tarinas Abon; his nine-year-old daughter, who was seasick all the way to Rongelap; Paul Kabua, son of Kwajalein *iroij* Imada Kabua; and Kenja Tambo. Kotak Loeak had left us at Majuro, embarrassed that his brother hadn't honoured a pledge to take his 25-metre fishing boat, *Takinal 5*, to help with the evacuation. So too, had Jolbo Samuel, who needed to get back to work at the Kwajalein Atoll Corporation office on Ebeye Island.

There were five journalists on board besides Fernando Pereira and myself. A French pair, Philippe Chatenay and Walter Guerin, were making a documentary to be screened in France on Hiroshima Day, when the *Warrior* would be bound for Moruroa. Gangling Chatenay, of *Le Point* news magazine, was flamboyantly talkative, speaking in an eastern American accent, while Parfrance television's Guerin had difficulty expressing himself in English.

Filing for the *Guardian* and *Washington Post* was the London newspaper's staff writer Paul Brown, a specialist in environmental affairs and well known among British Greenpeace campaigners. He was also making his first trip to the Pacific and delighted in writing anecdotes about tropical fish and swimming pigs. A Japanese freelance photo-journalist, Kousei Shimada, and television cameraman John Perulis, filming for Greenpeace Productions, rounded off the team. Shimada wanted to journey to Rongelap's northern islands in search of 'Gorgon-headed' coconut palms — radiation mutations that were reputedly there.

Giff Johnson couldn't leave his newspaper in Majuro initially, so he asked me to cover the early stages of the evacuation for the *Journal* until he joined us at Mejato.

The *Rainbow Warrior* arrived at Rongelap on 17 May. It was a paradise which fulfilled any dream of how a Pacific atoll in the tropic of cancer should be. Turquoise-coloured lagoon, coconut palms, searing sunshine, fish teeming in the reef and the scent of hibiscus blooms wafting in the air. And it is huge. The third-largest atoll in the Marshall Islands, Rongelap is roughly 80 kilometres across.

A village dominated by a white-plastered church with blue and pink facings skirted the beach of the main *motu*, or island. Five outrigger canoes sat idly on the coral sand. A grass airstrip cut through the palm trees with a 'Welcome to Rongelap' sign chipped into a trunk.

Did the islanders on this beautiful atoll really want to leave? The curse of Bravo seemed remote and the crew had uncertainties about their mission.

For months Steve Sawyer had been thinking out the details of moving all the islanders. Now he could see the village and it wàsn't just a couple of huts. It was a little township of about 320 people.

'Jesus, I don't believe it!' he said. 'People are leaving all this and going off to a place where there is nothing.'

It was disturbing to contemplate: the Rongelapese were prepared to disinherit themselves and face an uncertain future for the sake of their children.

This wasn't a game, nor the sort of publicity stunt that Greenpeace could do so successfully. It wasn't even a campaign in the sense of campaigns as understood by the ecology movement over the past 14 years. These were real people with real lives that the crew was now involved with.

Sawyer hoped they were up to it. He had plenty of confidence in the crew's ability to do the job physically. But he hoped it could be accomplished with little trauma.

Senator Jeton Anjain stood on the main deck, gazing shorewards. Julian Riklon was at his side, filming the welcome for a video he was making of the evacuation.

A *bum bum* headed out from shore to greet the

Right: *Fernando Pereira and Rongelap Islander Bonemej Namwe ride ashore in the* bum bum. *Born on Kwajalein, Namwe, 62, has lived most of her life on Rongelap. 'The United States use our people for studying as if we were chickens and pigs.'*

Rainbow Warrior. The small, rickety motor boat, one of two belonging to the islanders, was named from the Marshallese word mimicking the sound of its engine: *boom boom!*

As the boat got closer, and began circling the ship, we could see 11 women on board. Fluttering from the stern was a white cloth with words scrawled in red: 'We love the future of our kids'. The *Rainbow Warrior* with its big black 'Nuclear-free Pacific' banner seemed huge beside this vulnerable little boat with its handkerchief-sized flag.

As the women sang, tears stung the eyes of Grace O'Sullivan, Nathalie Mestre and Hanne Sorensen. Emotion tugged also at the hearts of the other crew. The islanders had a haunting style of singing through their noses which made their voices sound like bagpipes. Always with one singer sounding off key. It couldn't help but send shivers up our spines.

> *I love my home island, where I was born*
> *I will never leave it.*
> *This is my home, my only home*
> *And it is better that I die on it.*

When the *bum bum* bumped alongside the *Rainbow Warrior*, several Rongelapese women climbed on board. Senator Anjain and the other islanders were treated to embraces and kisses. Pereira and I leapt on to the boat to be taken ashore for the welcome ritual.

An archway of coconut timber and plaited pandanus leaves, sheathed in hibiscus flowers, stood on the beach. Across the arch was a striking banner: '*Ba eman kabjere* — We Love the Future of Our Kids!'

About 20 minutes later the first group from the crew arrived in a Zodiac inflatable speedboat. The *Warrior* women were clad in skirts hastily thrown over their workshorts. The crew were garlanded with *wu*, floral crowns, and sweet-scented leis, and treated to drinking coconuts as the island women sang their nasal welcome songs. Curiously, the village men stayed aloof from the welcome. Did they have doubts about leaving?

Chatenay and Guerin had missed the boat. When they finally arrived ashore in the Zodiac they tried to persuade the Rongelapese to re-enact the ritual. 'It's for a special film on French television,' pleaded Chatenay. But the women were not impressed.

A meeting was set for 2 p.m. so the villagers could talk with Senator Anjain and the crew. Any lingering uncertainty we had about the people wanting to evacuate faded as we wandered around the island. Several houses already had their roofs and walls stripped off. Corrugated aluminium sheeting and plywood were stacked in neat, labelled piles.

Rongelap Elementary School was almost completely

Right: *The partly demolished Rongelap Elementary School and head teacher Aisen Tima (left) with some of his pupils. 'It's obvious to me that our islands were used because the United States saw us as low-class.'*

demolished, desks and chairs scattered around the coral sand playground. About 75 children — a quarter of the population — went to the school. They were to have been given a new building by the Marshalls Education Ministry but now it would be at least a year or two before they got another school — if they got one at all.

'The school is already a wipe out,' said schoolteacher Aisen Tima, perched dejectedly on an old desk. 'If the weather is good on Mejato it will be possible for me to have classes under the trees.' Tima, 32, was among the first Rongelap Islanders to be flown to the United States for thyroid tumour surgery after radiation-linked illnesses began to emerge among the islanders.

It was 2 p.m. Henk Haazen and Bunny McDiarmid, still operating on European time, arrived at the shadehouse next to the church where the meeting was to be held, and sat down. Hardly anybody was there. An ominous sign, they thought.

But islanders began drifting in by twos and threes and by three o'clock, almost the whole village was there. The women sat on bench seats in the shadehouse; the men on gnarled roots of a giant breadfruit tree, or squatting on the coral sand.

Like many Marshallese meetings, it started off on a very sombre note. Everybody seemed depressed. Two brothers of former schoolteacher Billiet Edmond, who had written a vivid diary of the Bravo hydrogen-bomb blast in 1954, sat grim-faced under the tree.

Senator Anjain began. He introduced the *Warrior* crew and he spelled out the atoll's tragic legacy of deaths and illnesses from the Bravo fallout.

'American scientists have been lying to us for 30 years about the radiation on our islands,' he said. 'The poison from the Bravo monster bomb is still being felt today. Our people suffered then, and we are still suffering from radiation diseases such as thyroid tumours, cancer, leukemia, birth defects, stillbirths and miscarriages.

'Now, as we all decided last year, the time has come for us to leave for Mejato Island. For the sake of our children and our grandchildren.'

Not a stir among the men. But an elderly woman asked: 'How are we going to eat — there are few coconuts and no breadfruit growing on Mejato? How are we going to get money?'

'It will be hard, but we'll find a way to survive,' replied Anjain.

Now it was Julian Riklon's turn. 'We know it's going to be tough, trying to make a new life, to become alienated from our land and our spiritual roots. But we also have no choice. The future of our children is most important — by staying here they have no hope. They are bound to die from cancer.'

Riklon, 39, treasurer of the Kwajalein Atoll Corporation, had returned to his home atoll for the first time since 1960. He was one of a community of Rongelap Islanders living on Ebeye because they thought staying on the atoll was a potential death sentence. (Later, he told me he believed triggering the Bravo bomb was murder.)

A fisherman asked what was going to happen to his outrigger canoe. He was assured it would be taken to Mejato. Then somebody cracked a joke and suddenly it was all over. A logistics meeting between Anjain, Riklon, mayor Randy Thomas and other island leaders was set for the next afternoon with Sawyer, skipper Peter Willcox and first mate Gotje to fine tune Operation Exodus.

'The people looked to me to find a way to save them, but they didn't really believe a ship would come all the way from Britain,' said Anjain. 'It wasn't until they saw the *Rainbow Warrior* in their lagoon that they really believed me. They thought I might be bluffing.'

That evening, chief engineer Davey Edward, having missed the welcome, decided to go ashore. But if he was looking for a corner pub, he was to be disappointed. The island was dry, apart from *jakaro*, fermented coconut frond juice. All he could find were campfires and mosquitos. He spent the night on the beach under a pandanus tree.

Some of the crew, particularly deckhand Grace O'Sullivan, were worried about the level of residual radiation on Rongelap. How harmful was it? O'Sullivan, a powerfully built swimming champion, went ashore rather gingerly. Two years before in a Greenpeace campaign at Britain's nuclear reprocessing plant at Windscale, she had been contaminated. She had gone in a Zodiac inflatable to check an outflow pipe, spewing plutonium waste into the Irish Sea, to see if it could be plugged. The boat became surrounded by an oil-based detergent slick floating on the sea.

The electronic radiation detector shot off the scale and O'Sullivan headed back to the *Cedarlea* as fast as she could. On board she asked an electrical technician whether the detector was working properly. BEEP . . . BEEP . . . BEEP, it buzzed when held near her clothes. They nearly died with fright!

The ship returned to London, eight hours away. Next day she, her companion and the Zodiac were taken to the National Radiation Protection Board centre at Harwell for monitoring. Technicians in decontamination suits immediately roped them off with radioactive signs. 'Hot' readings were taken all over them, but the highest were on O'Sullivan's scarf and a pair of gloves belonging to her crewmate. Still, they were scrubbed down, decontaminated and told they were safe.

This time, O'Sullivan wasn't taking any chances. Sawyer had bought a radiation detector costing $200 from a solar electronics firm run by The Farm, a community near Summertown, Tennessee, to bring on the voyage. Called a 'nuke buster', it was the only sophisticated piece of electronic equipment on board apart from navigation and communications gear. It measured beta and gamma rays.

Andy Biedermann, the ship's doctor, took the detector ashore, but didn't find any risk readings. However, it wasn't really expected as the islands with serious residual radiation levels were in the north of the atoll — the islanders' traditional coconut crab larder.

On Sunday, 19 May, the Rongelapese gathered in their church for a last service before bolting the doors and leaving

the atoll. Decorations from the previous Christmas were still hanging inside the austere room.

'It is a sad moment,' said Pastor Jatai Mongkeyea. 'But remember what is happening to us is rather like the biblical deliverance of the Israelites from Egypt.' The women choir sang a tearful eulogy about their homeland, finishing with the Marshall Islands national anthem which says they would never leave their island.

Out of a church window we could see the village cemetery, a huddle of whitewashed headstones including the victims of radiation illnesses. The grave of Lekoj Anjain, Senator Anjain's nephew, was marked by a black plaque. Lekoj's father, John Anjain, polished it as a parting gesture.

The rest of the day was spent tearing down houses. Loading the *Rainbow Warrior* began in earnest on Monday. About 20 tonnes of building materials, two of three generators from the island, wooden trunks, furniture, kerosene lamps, tools and sleeping mats were ferried out to the ship in the *bum bums* and two Zodiacs.

Shortly before dusk, the first nuclear refugees were taken on board ready for the trip. About 75 mainly elderly people, pregnant women and mothers with young children squeezed into whatever space they could — including Biedermann and Edward's cabins. Gotje, second mate Bene Hoffmann and other crew slung a tarpaulin shelter over the

Left: *Rongelap Islanders preparing to leave.*

Right: *Islanders with their belongings approach the* Rainbow Warrior.

boat deck and many of the islanders huddled there. Others spread their mats in the carpentry shop. Real sailing was out because there was no deck room.

My report that night for Radio New Zealand's *Morning Report*, as the ship headed for Mejato, 160 kilometres south-eastwards, said:

> It's hard to make a guesstimate of how many people are on board the *Rainbow Warrior*. As she steams toward Mejato, the trawler seems packed with Rongelap islanders heading for a new home of hope. Most are sleeping on deck, but many have bunked down in the hold and some elderly people have found refuge in the mess room. It took two days to load the ship with building materials from demolished houses, clothes, mats and trunks full of gear. Many of the trunks bear labels from the Brookhaven National Laboratory, the clinic monitoring the islanders' health since the Bravo fallout 31 years ago.

By the time we reached Mejato next morning after 14 hours at sea, the ship's radio telephone was running hot with calls for 'Gulf Sierra Zulu Yankee', our high seas code. Operator Lloyd Anderson had already moved his bunk to the radio room and now he was working hard to keep

Left: *Islanders with their belongings pack a* bum bum *on the way out to the* Warrior. *On the left is Japanese photo-journalist Hiro Toyosaki. On the right is the atoll's mayor, Randy Thomas.*

Right: *Steve Sawyer brings islanders to the* Warrior *in a Zodiac.*

Greenpeace offices in London and Washington, international news agencies and newspapers posted with details.

A telex-computer link between the *Warrior* and Greenpeace's radio station in San Francisco, operated by Dick Dillman, was also used for communications. But it developed a terminal condensation 'disease', much to the annoyance of Paul Brown and myself when stories we filed vanished.

A banner headline in the *Pacific Daily News* said simply: Atoll Evacuation Begins'.

Senator Anjain and Julian Riklon were cited by the newspaper as appealing for help 'to meet our basic needs'. Anjain condemned the United States for refusing assistance, and Riklon said: 'We hope that people around the world will make the evacuation of Rongelap as painless as possible.'

The exodus became front-page news from the *Guardian* in London to *De Volksrant* in Amsterdam. Pereira's photographs for Associated Press wire service were even splashed in papers such as Hong Kong's *South China Morning Post*. Yet the drama went unnoticed by the New Zealand press, except in my reports to the *New Zealand Times*.

Giff Johnson met us at Mejato after a 120-kilometre trip from Ebeye in a speedboat. Later, Glenn Alcalay, who had just presented a report to the United Nations Trusteeship Council condemning Washington's policies in Micronesia, also joined us. He had originally been sceptical about the evacuation, but was now an enthusiastic advocate.

Also on board now was another Japanese freelance photo-journalist, Hiro Toyosaki, whom I had met a couple of years earlier in Port Vila. He had lived in an old dispensary on Rongelap, documenting the islanders' last 40 days on the atoll. And he had interviewed everyone.

Mejato, previously uninhabited and handed over to the people of Rongelap by their close relatives on nearby Ebadon Island, was a lot different to their own island. It was beautiful, but it was only three kilometres long and a kilometre wide, with a dry side and a dense tropical side. A sandspit joined it to another small, uninhabited island. Although lush, Mejato was uncultivated and already it was apparent there could be a food problem.

Out on the shallow reef, fish were plentiful. Shortly after the *Warrior* arrived, several of the men were out wading knee-deep on the coral spearing fish for lunch.

But even the shallowness of the reef caused a problem. It made it dangerous to bring the *Warrior* any closer than about three kilometres offshore — as two shipwrecks on the reef reminded us.

The cargo of building materials and belongings had to be laboriously unloaded on to a *bum bum*, which had also travelled overnight with no navigational aids apart from a Marshallese 'wave map', and the Zodiacs. It took two days to unload the ship with a swell making things difficult

Right: *Rongelap Islanders on board the* Rainbow Warrior *bound for Mejato.*

at times. An 18-year-old islander fell into the sea between the *bum bum* and the *Warrior*, almost being crushed but escaping with a jammed foot.

The delayed return to Rongelap for the next load didn't trouble Davey Edward. In fact, he was celebrating his first fishing success on the reef after almost three months of catching nothing. He finally landed not only a red snapper, but a dozen fish, including a half-metre shark! Edward was also a good cook and he rustled up dinner — shark montfort, snapper fillets, tuna steaks and salmon pie (made from cans of dumped American aid food salmon the islanders didn't want).

Returning to Rongelap, the *Rainbow Warrior* was confronted with a load which seemed double that taken on the first trip. Altogether, about 100 tonnes of building materials and other supplies were shipped to Mejato. The crew packed as much as they could on deck and left for Mejato, this time with 114 people on board. And it was a rough voyage with almost everybody being seasick.

The journalists were roped in to clean up the ship before returning to Rongelap on the third journey.

Alcalay, who spoke Marshallese, was a great help to me interviewing some of the islanders. 'It's a hard time for us now because we don't have a lot of food here on Mejato — like breadfruit, taro and pandanus,' said Rose Keju, who wasn't actually at Rongelap during the fallout. 'Our people

Left: On board the Warrior *during the second trip to Mejato.*

feel extremely depressed. They see no light, only darkness. They've been crying a lot.

'We've moved because of the poison and the health problems we face. If we have honest scientists check Rongelap we'll know whether we can ever return, or we'll have to stay on Mejato.'

Kiosang Kios, now 46, was 15 years old at the time of Bravo when she was evacuated to 'Kwaj'. 'My hair fell out — about half the people's hair fell out,' she said. 'My feet ached and burned. I lost my appetite, had diarrhoea and vomited.'

In 1957 she had her first baby and it was born without bones — 'like this paper, it was flimsy'. A so-called 'jellyfish baby', it lived half a day. After that, Kios had several more miscarriages and stillbirths. In 1959 she had a daughter who has problems with her legs and feet, and thyroid trouble.

Out on the reef, with the *bum bums*, the islanders had a welcome addition — an unusual hardwood dugout canoe being used for fishing and transport. It came 13,000 kilometres on board the *Rainbow Warrior* and bore the Sandinista legend FSLN on its black-and-red hull. A gift from McDiarmid and Haazen, it had been bought for $30 from a Nicaraguan fisherman while they were crewing on the *Fri*.

'It has come from a small people struggling for their sovereignty against the United States and it has gone to another small people doing the same,' said Haazen.

Before the 10-day evacuation ended, Haazen was given an outrigger canoe by the islanders. Winched on to the deck of the *Warrior*, it didn't quite make a sail-in protest at Moruroa, as Haazen planned, but it has since become a familiar sight on Auckland Harbour.

With the third load shipped to Mejato and one more to go, another problem emerged. What should be done about the scores of pigs and chickens on Rongelap? Pens could be built on the main deck to transport them to Mejato but was there any fodder left for them?

The islanders decided they weren't going to run a risk, no matter how slight, of having contaminated animals with them. They were abandoned on Rongelap — along with three of the five outriggers.

'When you get to New Zealand you'll be asked have you been on a farm,' warned Chatenay, who had gone there a few weeks before to prepare a *Le Point* article about the Land of the Long White Cloud and Nuclear-Free Nuts.

'Yes, and you'll be asked to remove your shoes. And if you don't have shoes, you'll be asked to remove your feet,' added Gotje, who was usually barefooted.

The last voyage was the most fun. A small group of about 40 islanders was transported and there was plenty of time to get to know each other.

Four young men questioned cook Nathalie Mestre: where did she live? Where was Switzerland? Out came an atlas. Then Mestre produced a scrapbook of Pereira's photographs of the voyage. The questions were endless.

They asked for a scrap of paper and a pen and wrote in English:

We, the people of Rongelap, love our homeland. But how can our people live in a place which is dangerous and poisonous. I mean, why didn't those American people test Bravo in a state capital? Why? *Rainbow Warrior*, thank you for being so nice to us. Keep up your good work.

Each one wrote down his name: Balleain Anjain, Ralet Anitak, Kiash Tima and Isaac Edmond. They handed the paper to Mestre and she added her name. Anitak grabbed it and wrote as well: 'Nathalie Anitak'.

Thursday, 30 May, was Fernando Pereira's thirty-fifth birthday. The evacuation was over and a one-day holiday was declared as we lay anchored off Mejato. Pereira was on the Pacific voyage almost by chance. Sawyer had been seeking a wire machine for transmitting pictures of the campaign. He phoned Fiona Davies, then heading the Greenpeace photo office in Paris. But he wanted a machine and photographer separately.

'No, no . . . I'll get you a wire machine,' replied Davies. 'But you'll have to take my photographer with it.' Agreed. The deal would save the campaign budget about $8,000.

Sawyer wondered who this guy was, although Gotje and some of the others knew him. Pereira had fled Portugal about 15 years before while he was serving as a pilot in the armed forces at a time when the country was fighting to retain colonies like Angola and Mozambique. He settled in Holland, the only country which would grant him citizenship. After first working as a photographer for Anefo press agency, he became concerned with environmental and social issues. Eventually he joined the Amsterdam communist daily *De Waarheid* and was assigned to cover the activities of Greenpeace. Later he joined Greenpeace.

Although he adopted Dutch ways, his charming Latin temperament and looks betrayed his Portuguese origins. He liked tight Italian-style clothes and fast sports cars. Pereira was always wide-eyed, happy and smiling. In Hawaii, he and Sawyer hiked up to the crater at the top of Diamond Head one day. Sawyer took a snapshot of Pereira laughing — a photo later used on the front page of the *New Zealand Times* after his death.

While most of the crew were taking things quietly and the 'press gang' caught up on stories, Sawyer led a mini-expedition in a Zodiac to one of the shipwrecks, the *Palauan Trader*. With him were Edward, Haazen, Paul Brown and McDiarmid.

Clambering on board the hulk, Sawyer grabbed hold of a rust-caked railing which collapsed. He plunged 10 metres in to a hold. While he lay in pain with a dislocated shoulder and severely lacerated abdomen, his crewmates smashed a hole through the side of the ship. They dragged him through pounding surf into the Zodiac and headed back to the *Warrior* three kilometres away.

'Doc' Biedermann, assisted by 'nurse' Chatenay, who had received basic medical training during national service in France, treated Sawyer. He took almost two weeks to recover.

But the accident failed to completely dampen celebrations for Pereira, who was presented with a hand-painted T-shirt labelled 'Rainbow Warrior Removals Inc'.

Pereira's birthday was the first of three which strangely coincided with events casting a tragic shadow over the *Rainbow Warrior's* last voyage.

CHAPTER FIVE

The Kwajalein Capers

Kwajalein Atoll may have contributed more to the
nuclear arms race than any other spot on earth.
— Author Giff Johnson

ONLY THE picturesque, whitewashed church with blue-and-pink facings was left standing untouched in the village on Rongelap Atoll. It was padlocked and shuttered, waiting for the day when the islanders might be able to return to their homeland. On tiny Mejato, their new home, there was a Robinson Crusoe atmosphere with piles of building materials dumped along the beach and packing trunks floated ashore across the reef from the *Rainbow Warrior*. Mattresses were sodden from tropical squalls. As the islanders got on with the task of building temporary shelters and a new village, a political storm blew up.

Ambassador Harvey Feldman, United States representative to the United Nations Trusteeship Council, told the council the exodus had been instigated by outsiders who had misled the islanders about radioactive contamination on the atoll. The Guam-based *Pacific Daily News* carried a banner headline: 'No Need To Flee Atoll, Says US'.

Feldman said there was 'simply no new scientific information, either radiologically or medically' which supported the move. But the ambassador, as the *Marshall Islands Journal* noted almost gleefully, was a former official of the Atomic Energy Commission, the agency accused by the islanders for their leukemia deaths, thyroid trouble, miscarriages and other health disorders after the 1954 Bravo blast. How could he be impartial?

The newspaper, however, was mistaken. Aged 23 at the time of Bravo, Feldman had been employed only by the State Department since he graduated in Oriental language and literature at the University of Chicago.

The ambassador told the council it was a 'tragic' case of misinformation. He claimed the Rongelapese, by eating locally grown food on the atoll, would be exposed to less radiation than people living in Denver, Colorado. Feldman said people living in Washington, DC, received about 150 millirems of radiation — about double the exposure of islanders on Wotho Atoll, 160 kilometres south of Rongelap. Radiation standards in the United States state that an individual should receive no more than 500 millirems a year, a far more relaxed standard than in many countries.

'The administering authority feels that it is tragic that

the people of Rongelap have been victimised by outside forces without the benefit of the available scientific information,' Feldman said.

The attack stung usually mild-mannered Senator Jeton Anjain, Rongelap's representative in the *Nitijela*, into an angry counterblast. Anjain denied the evacuation had been prompted by Greenpeace or anybody else:

It was instigated by me and my people as a result of the American nuclear testing programme. Secondly, we don't need the most brilliant scientists to come and tell us we're not sick. We know we have had health problems on Rongelap from the beginning — we are having them today and we will have them for the indefinite future. If the United States thinks that my people are okay, why should they come twice a year to use them as guinea pigs?

In an open letter published by the *Pacific Daily News* and *Marshall Islands Journal*, Greenpeace coordinator Steve Sawyer added:

Ambassador Feldman is correct when he says that 'the people of Rongelap have been victimised by outside forces'. The United States Government has been victimising the people of Rongelap with radioactive fallout, 'tragic misinformation' and outright lies since 1946. His suggestion that Greenpeace instigated the evacuation is ludicrous on the face of it to anyone even remotely aware of the actual situation, especially considering that the evacuation has had the approval of the *Nitijela* for nearly two years. . . . The

suggestion that the Marshall Islands Government didn't know about the evacuation in advance should let everyone here in the Marshalls know what a lot of ignorant bureaucrats live in Washington, DC. Who do they think they are trying to fool?

The second salvo from the United States Government came with claims it had not been advised of the move and it had been told by the Marshall Islands Government Mejato Island had plenty of food for the Rongelap Islanders.

A food shortage for the Rongelap people reflected badly on both governments. Midway through the evacuation several families ran out of rice and flour (relied on as staple foods since the people had been warned about contamination on the northern islets of their atoll). Relatives began sending supplies by speedboat from Ebeye Island, 120 kilometres away at the southern end of Kwajalein Atoll. The government field ship *Militobi*, already more than six weeks late, was still scheduled to go to Rongelap with supplies of United States surplus aid food, even though it would have arrived there after the islanders had left.

The food supply for the Rongelapese looked as though it would run out within a few days. The previously uninhabited island was uncultivated and, although fish out on the reef were plentiful, no outrigger canoes had yet been delivered. Julian Riklon's brother Johnsay, a lawyer, accused his government of being prepared to let the islanders starve.

Guardian reporter Paul Brown and I spoke to Foreign Affairs Minister Tony deBrum by radio telephone from the

Rainbow Warrior and he assured us action would be taken. Anjain later phoned the skipper of the *Militobi*, which was unloading at Ebeye, and asked him to come to Mejato. The ship brought food to the island two days later and then continued its voyage around the northern atolls. But the journalists and crew on the *Warrior* found it hard to believe the islanders could be abandoned by both governments.

The Marshalls Government was upset by US Interior Department official Larry Morgan, who claimed neither government had been given warning of the move. The claim lacked any credibility in the face of Senator Anjain's approaches to Congress for help. In fact, the congressional public lands sub-committee had even voted for $300,000 to be allocated to an independent radiological survey — something the Rongelapese had been seeking for years — and $3.2 million for resettling if the survey rules Rongelap unsafe for habitation.

Rongelap leaders accused the United States Government of launching a campaign to discredit the evacuation. They described Morgan's claim as misleading and cited the unanimous resolution by the *Nitijela* in August 1983, which included a request to Washington to 'provide . . . adequate funding for the resettlement of the people of Rongelap in some other place of their choice which is safe and free from contamination'. The resolution asked the Marshall Islands Government to take action to seek United States support. Also, Interior Department officials had listened to a series of Rongelapese delegates testifying in congressional hearings about their plans to evacuate their atoll since early in 1984.

Leaving Mejato was an emotional wrench. Many of the crew wanted to remain on the island, help build houses and get the generators going. Andy Biedermann wanted to do more for the ill; he had found evidence of tuberculosis among the children. But they realised they had accomplished all they could for the moment and there was still the rest of the Pacific campaign ahead.

The *Rainbow Warrior* weighed anchor and sailed for Ebeye Island. On board were John Anjain, several pregnant women and mothers with children going to seek medical treatment at the overtaxed, understaffed local hospital.

I asked one of the islanders how to write the word *el*, raw fish marinated in coconut cream.

'It starts with E,' she replied, and added with a chuckle: 'You know, like in *ex*-posed to radiation.'

When the ship arrived at Ebeye, most of the crew spent a wild night dancing at the Monkubok Bar and the Happy Islander disco. Fernando Pereira danced almost non-stop until just before dawn. He was still celebrating his birthday.

The Rongelap Islanders living on Ebeye hosted a traditional feast at the home of *iroij* Michael Kabua in appreciation for the crew's help in the evacuation. Before the islanders left for home, they passed a collection basket around for a gift, rather like the Maori koha custom. They filed past the crew, shaking hands. Such was their humility and shyness that chief engineer Davey Edward was moved

Right: *The four excavation voyages from Rongelap Atoll to Mejato Island on Kwajalein Atoll.*

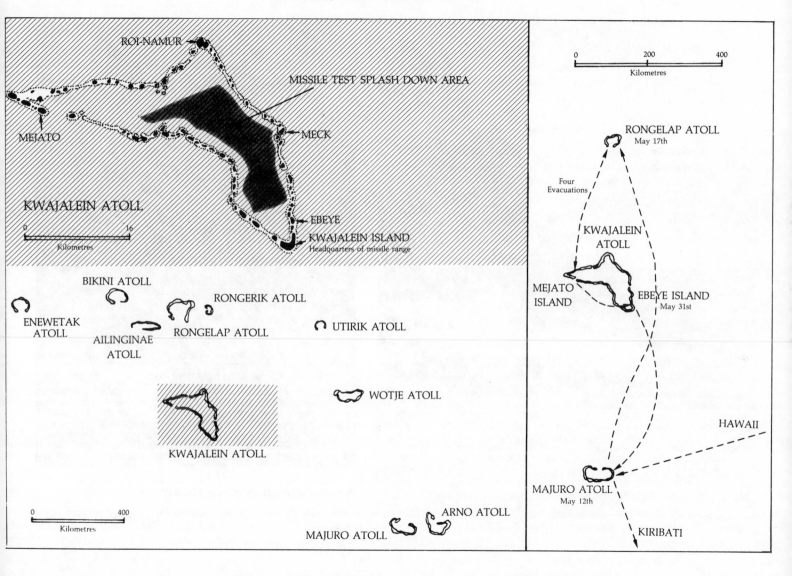

ROI-NAMUR

MISSILE TEST SPLASH DOWN AREA

MECK

MEJATO

KWAJALEIN ATOLL

0   16
Kilometres

EBEYE
KWAJALEIN ISLAND
Headquarters of missile range

BIKINI ATOLL

RONGERIK ATOLL

ENEWETAK
ATOLL

AILINGINAE
ATOLL

RONGELAP ATOLL

UTIRIK ATOLL

WOTJE ATOLL

KWAJALEIN ATOLL

0   400
Kilometres

ARNO ATOLL

MAJURO ATOLL

0   200   400
Kilometres

RONGELAP ATOLL
May 17th

Four
Evacuations

KWAJALEIN
ATOLL

MEJATO
ISLAND

EBEYE ISLAND
May 31st

HAWAII

MAJURO ATOLL
May 12th

KIRIBATI

Above: *Makeshift shelter on Mejato.*

Left: *Building materials dumped on the beach at Mejato.*

to tears. Embarrassed, the crew were uncertain what to do with the $90 koha. Should it be spent on a memento of the Marshall Islands for the *Warrior*? Instead, the crew decided on a special Chinese dinner together, except for Edward who bought a traditional Marshallese plaited-pandanus basket.

It was time to farewell journalists Philippe Chatenay, Walter Guerin and Paul Brown. I was staying on board until Auckland. Glenn Alcalay also caught the ferry to Kwajalein Island to fly back to the United States.

'When I saw the film of Neville Shute's book *On the Beach* at the age of 12 I had a nightmare that night,' he told me before leaving. 'It wasn't until years later that I realised it was Bravo and the Marshall Islands that inspired Shute.'

On the day Alcalay returned to Washington, he was hassled by the FBI. An FBI agent phoned him and said he had evidence Alcalay had been talking to somebody in the Soviet Embassy about Micronesia and the Compact, and asked him to talk about it. In fact, Alcalay had merely had lunch with an embassy secretary and discussed the trusteeship in casual terms.

Alcalay told the FBI agent he wasn't interested in talking.

'I find it peculiar that you will talk with *them*, but not with us,' the agent sneered. Alcalay hung up.

On 10 June 1984 a United States missile with a dummy nuclear warhead streaked above the Pacific into space. Seven thousand kilometres away another missile was fired from Kwajalein Atoll and caught the warhead with an infra-red homing system. An umbrellalike device, five metres wide, unfolded and rammed the dummy in a spectacular explosion that flashed across sensor screens.

It was a dramatic glimpse of Star Wars in action — the first time in military history a warhead had been destroyed 160 kilometres out in space. 'Just like hitting a bullet with a bullet,' said a Pentagon official. The 'killer' device was fired from Meck Island on the atoll. It intercepted the warhead fired from a Minuteman III launched from Vandenberg Air Force base in southern California.

Kwajalein Missile Range, the former military support base in the 1940s and 1950s when the United States triggered 66 nuclear bombs in the Marshall Islands, and its $1,000 million facilities are the cornerstone of President Reagan's controversial Strategic Defence Initiative research. It is also the 'bullseye' for intercontinental ballistic missile testing and a vital part of the American deep-space tracking capabilities. The new MX missiles are also tested there.

'Kwajalein has been the primary range for testing the accuracy of intercontinental ballistic missiles and for developing anti-ballistic missile systems combining radar, infra-red sensors, computers and interceptor rockets,' wrote Giff Johnson in his book *Collision Course at Kwajalein*.[1] 'A more recent development has catapulted the Marshall Islands to the forefront of the nuclear conflict. For the first time, Kwajalein is a high-priority nuclear target since the Altair radar on Roi-Namur Island went online for early warning and anti-satellite space tracking operations in 1982.'

Kwajalein has been surrounded for years by a storm of controversy and lawsuits. Its development has created squalid conditions for almost 9,000 Marshallese packed like sardines on to 33-hectare Ebeye Island.

The 'ghetto of the Pacific', as the plywood-shanty island has been labelled, would have been regarded as an international scandal if the islanders were Palestinian or Vietnamese refugees, and not a small ethnic group tucked away on a remote atoll. More than two-thirds of the islanders belong to families forced by the United States to move from islets throughout the atoll about 20 years before to make room for the missile tests.[2] The rest come from other atolls in search of work at the base.

However, less than 900 Ebeye people actually have regular jobs, about two-thirds working for about $3.50 an hour on the base.[3] Conditins on Ebeye and United States rent payments have long been a source of dispute. In 1982 a four-month-long islander sail-in protest dubbed Operation Homecoming forced the United States military to promise about $15 million to improve Ebeye's facilities. As a result of that protest the Kwajalein Atoll Corporation, a land rights movement, has forced the payment of an annual rent of $9 million. But now the islanders want to double the lease payments and to have them paid directly to them instead of the Marshalls Government.

'I would like to see any United States military activity on Kwajalein restricted to purely conventional American naval or air forces,' said Senator Ataji Balos, a leader of the KAC.

A half-hour ferry ride from Ebeye is 302-hectare Kwajalein Island. Kwajalein, the oddest island in the Pacific, bristles with huge radar dishes and radio antennae among the coconut palms. Its airstrip is capable of landing the world's largest aircraft and it houses a luxury town of 3,000 expatriates whose suburbs are typically American.

There is one nine-hole golf course, baseball fields, a bowling alley, two swimming pools and a fully staffed hospital (which Ebeye Islanders cannot generally use). The equipment on Kwajalein is impressive — giant radar dishes pumping out 400 million watts; telescopes which can track a missile 3,000 kilometres away travelling at 28,000 kilometres an hour; even a high-tech video camera used in filming Hollywood's blockbuster *Star Wars*.

Only about 30 of the community's population are military staff, even though the base is run by the United States Army. Most of the rest are engineers, technicians and other civilian workers, some with their families. Even the large police force is run by a private security company.

Journalists are virtually banned on Kwajalein. Getting official clearance to go there is rare and when reporters do visit they create a stir.

Having tried in vain to get permission to visit from the United States Embassy before leaving New Zealand for the

Right: *Space-age radar domes and monitoring equipment on Roi-Namur Island, Kwajalein Atoll. The Altair space-tracking radar is the giant dish on the right.*

Marshall Islands ('Kwajalein? What's that?' asked the official), I attempted to visit the base anyway.

Armed with an introductory letter from a Pacific news magazine for the commanding officer, Colonel William Spin, I caught the 6.45 a.m. ferry from Ebeye. Stepping off the boat on Kwajalein Island, I was confronted with a barbed wire fence bearing the Marshallese words 'Jab Ella Jen Line In' (Police barrier: Don't proceed beyond this point).

Four armed security police immediately surrounded me as I explained I wanted to speak to a liaison officer to arrange a meeting with the colonel. (The base couldn't be phoned from Ebeye).

'Er, we don't allow journalists here,' said the liaison officer. But he agreed to talk to Spin.

While waiting for the colonel's reply, I chatted with one of the guards, Don Smith, a Vietnam War veteran and a former mercenary security guard in the Middle East. 'New Zealand, eh?' he said. 'That's the country that's gone all commie and banned our ships. Don't like your kind.'

He had no real grasp of New Zealand's nuclear-free policies, which include a prohibition on visits by nuclear-armed or powered ships to its ports while remaining part of the Western alliance. In a friendlier tone, he turned his attention to the islanders coming off the ferry: 'They don't know how bloody well off they are here. If the United States left "Kwaj", they would only lease it out to somebody else — and that would be the commies.'

'It's far better that the United States remains here,' said Smith. 'We give them freedom; we don't interfere·

'Look at the ferry. It has a canteen and the Marshallese workers can have a cup of coffee or something when they come over. And when the boat goes back it sells cut-price beer, so they're pretty happy really.'

Although there is about one policeman for every five people in Kwajalein, security isn't much of a problem. 'The worst thing for us is a bicycle theft,' Smith said. 'Well, it's not really stealing. People just borrow somebody else's bike.

'One thing that isn't tolerated is any hint of violence. If somebody strikes somebody else they're on a plane back to the United States in a flash.'

The liaison officer was back with Colonel Spin's answer. 'No, the commander says it's impossible. He's not talking to journalists. In any case, you would have to go through the New Zealand Embassy in Washington and they would have to seek clearance from Huntsville, Alabama.' (The Ballistic Missile Defense Systems Command is based in Huntsville.)

In spite of the crude contrast between Kwajalein and Ebeye, things are changing — gradually. A young, confident leadership on the atoll has been negotiating with the Pentagon for a fairer deal.

'The people of Ebeye realise the colonel isn't God anymore,' said Ben Barry, a former United States serviceman now exiled on Ebeye. He writes a lively weekly column about life on the island in the *Marshall Islands Journal*.

With the election of 31-year-old Alvin Jacklick as the first Ebeye mayor in 1983, the KAC has made considerable progress in improving conditions. A draft development plan was drawn up and two years later a progress report said:

> Substantial improvement has been made. The power plant has been rehabilitated, the fresh water distribution system replaced and a water treatment plant constructed. The sewage plant is now operational. . . . The hospital has been rehabilitated. It now has usable operating rooms, working toilets, new windows and a repaired roof which keeps out the salt spray.

Jacklick was on a State Department junket while I was on Ebeye, but I was able to speak to one of his key lieutenants. Chief clerk Abon Jeadrik, 29, sat in an office which had walls plastered with a 'Kwajalein Atoll — Nuclear-Free Zone' poster and clippings about independence in the Pacific. In 1984 he was one of two Marshallese delegates to the Nuclear-Free and Independent Pacific movement meeting in Australia.

'The government in Majuro calls us a bunch of radicals,' Jeadrik said. 'But what they don't like is that we're running the show from Ebeye.'

For years, the Marshalls Government has neglected Ebeye, even though more than a quarter of the country's population lives there.[4] It has preferred to let the United States military solve problems, an attitude which has angered Ebeye leaders.

'There isn't any point waiting for authority from Majuro,' Jeadrik said. 'If we ask for action they don't do anything, so we might as well get on with it ourselves.' The Ebeye administration has filed a lawsuit against the government for failing to honour a pledge to pay the salaries of 12 police on the island.

Ebeye is certainly the stronghold of Opposition politicians in the *Nitijela* — men like Senators Ataji Balos and Imada Kabua, a cousin of the Marshalls President, Amata Kabua. The Ebeye leadership set the precedent of hiring lawyers to wage legal battles against the United States military authorities. More than 3,000 Marshallese have followed the example by filing lawsuits against the United States Government, seeking almost $5,000 million in compensation for the nuclear tests in the Marshall Islands.

As the end of the territory's trust status approaches, Congress has recently concluded a lengthy series of hearings for the Compact of Free Association. Although it is the product of more than 15 years of difficult negotiations, the treaty is regarded by many Marshallese as having serious deficiencies that will give Micronesia an uncertain status in its relationship with the United States. Under the Compact's section 177 'espousal' clause, the islanders would be stripped of their rights to press the lawsuits.

Jeadrik described some of Ebeye's plans for the future. The United States Government is contributing about half the $15 million needed to build a causeway linking Ebeye to seven islets in the north as far as Ninge. This will more than quadruple the land available and ease the overcrowding. Other United States grants approved include $500,000 for emergency repairs to a New Zealand-built dock, and $1 million to cover a shortfall for a power and desalination plant now being built. About $2.25 million will also be spent on a third generator to be used as a power backup for Ebeye. A secondary school is planned, on an island which doesn't have one even though half the population is under the age of 16.

Many of the islanders resent the 'arrogant and racist' attitude of the military administration on Kwajalein Island and of the American community.

'What upsets us deeply is that we're treated as prisoners on our own land,' complained Julian Riklon.

A bunker in the heart of the island was built 20 years before in case of mishaps with missiles. But as one Ebeye Islander said: 'It could hardly keep out the pop from a pop gun!' The building is now used as a school and a studio for a local cable television station.

In spite of the enormous problems, the island's leaders are confident about the future. *Iroij* Michael Kabua, a 40-year-old businessman and brother of Senator Imada Kabua, said plans to spend $140 million over the next five years on 'basic' improvements could point the way for development on other Pacific atolls. Jeadrik agreed. 'I see Ebeye one day becoming a model island town for the Marshalls, if not the Pacific.'

Most Americans on Kwajalein, Meck or Roi-Namur Islands are unaware of the squalid conditions on Ebeye. Yet some are privately critical of the US administration as this poem shows:

We can't voice our opinion,
Our phone lines are tapped,
With one patrolman for five
We've a feeling we're trapped.
Base living it's called
But one wonders for who;
It's more like an encampment
With 'who' watching 'you'.

Lijon Eknilang was aged seven at the time of Bravo. Now she is 38. She had long ago left Rongelap Atoll, fleeing to Ebeye in the hope of a healthier life. She recently made a statement to a congressional subcommittee as a traditional landowner on Ailingnae Atoll, near Rongelap, on the plight of her people.

'Like many of our women exposed during the bomb tests, I have had many miscarriages – seven,' she says. 'I have lived in fear and I feel my life is in danger. I sometimes feel my body is on fire.'

Miscarriages used to be rare on Rongelap. If a woman had one, her companions would sit with her all night long, or for three or four days. They would be afraid.

'Now miscarriages happen all the time. We take them for granted,' Eknilang said. 'We never used to have problems with mentally retarded children, or youngsters with stunted growth. Now it is a frequent problem. There have been at least six or seven jellyfish babies — they have no face. They have short bodies, stubby legs and look fat and shapeless. They live for half a day or so and then die.

'Losing my homeland really hurts. It's a pain that hurts

me here in my heart terribly. It is sad for our children. They'll grow up hearing about our traditional home but I don't know if they'll ever be able to go back there.

'It's easy for the Americans in Washington to say there is no problem. They don't have to cope with it. We are suffering from radiation every day of our lives. We appeal to the United States to look into our problems with a humane conscience.'

Protesting at Kwajalein presented a problem for the *Rainbow Warrior* crew. It was important that they made the connection between Star Wars, missile tests and nuclear fallout victims like the Rongelap islanders but they had to do it without risking arrests or seizure of the ship. The *Warrior* had to get to Moruroa.

Also, it was important the islanders on Ebeye knew the protest was not intended to threaten their dependency on the missile range for jobs. It was one thing for the islanders to stage their own sail-in which was mainly over the terms of the lease. But it was another for foreigners to make a protest which could be interpreted as an attack on their jobs. The crew realised one mistake could damage the enormous goodwill which had been gained during the evacuation.

Sailing the *Warrior* into the small Kwajalein military harbour, just across the channel from Ebeye, protesting on the military-run ferries, or crewmembers chaining themselves to the heavily guarded main gate were rejected as forms of protest.

Instead, a Zodiac set off at dawn on 6 June with mate Bene Hoffmann at the tiller. On board were Bunny McDiarmid, Grace O'Sullivan and Andy Biedermann with a 10-metre wide banner made the day before. The inflatable was beached near the harbour on Kwajalein Island and the trio scaled a protective fence around a giant radar dome and unfurled the banner, which said: 'Kemij Jab Maron Lomoren Aolep Ri Lol' (We cannot relocate the world — stop Star Wars).

They had difficulty attaching the banner and were up the fence for a long time. An elderly American couple, out for a morning stroll, looked up and called out, 'Good morning'. It took 20 minutes for the security police to realise what was happening. They raced to the fence in two cars, and a helicopter swooped down but the Zodiac had escaped with the banner captured on television film and still photographs.

The *Auckland Star* carried an inaccurate front-page report of the protest. It said:

Greenpeace protesters, including two Aucklanders, have breached American security by entering ballistic missile range on Kwajalein, in the Pacific. Members of the *Rainbow Warrior's* crew, including Aucklanders Bunny McDiarmid and journalist David Robie, placed a banner protesting at America's presence in the Marshall Islands. They were observed by military personnel but no arrests were made.

In fact I wasn't there and I have never belonged to

Greenpeace. The paper later ran an apology. My story on Radio New Zealand said:

> Anti-nuclear protesters have 'invaded' an American missile base on Kwajalein Atoll, in the Marshall Islands. The three protesters, including a New Zealander, Bunny McDiarmid, are from the Greenpeace protest boat *Rainbow Warrior*. The protesters scaled a security fence and managed to elude security police while erecting a banner protesting at President Reagan's Star Wars programme. Security police swooped on the protesters as they fled from the atoll in a rubber liferaft, but no arrests were made.

The crew printed a pamphlet in Marshallese with a photograph of the protest which explained why they had demonstrated. They handed them out among the Ebeye Islanders, who thought the protest an admirable joke. The *Marshall Islands Journal* also ran a photograph.

Embarrassed military officials at the base told the Associated Press news agency in Honolulu the protest had taken place on the island's 'golf course'.

'Of course, what is really going on is that we have embarrassed the hell out of the KMR by spending 20 minutes in their "high security" area before they even knew we were there,' said Steve Sawyer, who had almost recovered from his shipwreck injuries.

However, a similar protest mounted two days later at Roi-Namur, the base's twin space-tracking islands, was rebuffed by tighter security.

Two days after the *Rainbow Warrior* left Kwajalein, a red flag was hoisted on Ebeye Wharf to warn islanders not to go into the splashdown zone and the United States test-fired another MX missile at the atoll.

Left: *The protest banner hoisted by three protesters from the* Warrior *on the protective fence around a Kwajalein radar dome.* (Fernando Pereira)

Footnotes to Chapter Five

1. Giff Johnson, *Collision Course at Kwajalein: Marshall Islanders in the Shadow of the Bomb*, Pacific Concerns Resource Centre, 1984.
2. In 1951 about 550 workers living on Kwajalein Island were moved into housing for 370 people. In 1964-5 400 people on islands in the splashdown zone were shifted to Ebeye and housed in concrete block units and given $25 a month 'compensation'. It was increased to $40 a month when the islanders complained. In 1964, years after they had been moved off their island, the Kwajalein Islanders were given $750,000 for signing a 99-year lease ($4 a hectare). They had no lawyers and were already displaced from their land. The Bikini and Enewetak people were treated similarly after their resettlement.
3. Although outsiders consider this US minimum wage low, it is two to three times above the Marshallese wage scale in Majuro or on Ebeye. It represents the lowest pay given to KMR workers, but this has still lured many islanders to Ebeye.
4. Kwajalein is the power base for the Marshall Islands in its relations with the US. The Kwajalein people believe that it is their right to deal directly with the US because it is their land, although the national Government in Majuro uses Kwajalein as its bargaining lever with the US. Many Kwajalein Islanders feel the national Government does not represent their interests.

CHAPTER SIX

From Majuro to Marsden Wharf

*Small is beautiful, peace is powerful, respect is honourable
and a sense of community is both wise and practical.*
—Father Walter Lini

IN THE *Rainbow Warrior's* chart room was a strip from the cartoon 'Hagar the Horrible'. As a Viking boat clung perilously to the edge of the ocean and a smoking hell opened up below, Hagar says: 'Okay . . . let's look at that map again'. Leaving Majuro behind on 13 June and sailing through the Fordyee channel past Arno, the 'atoll of love', to Kiribati the cartoon strip seemed to capture the feelings of the crew.

After departing from Kwajalein, the ship had returned to Majuro to prepare for the long trip to New Zealand. A problem had developed with the water-making machine in the engineroom. It appeared close to breakdown with a perished fanbelt. Could another belt be found? Chief engineer Davey Edward combed spare-parts yards in Majuro without luck. However, another crewman discovered one among the junk littering the beach.

'It's perfect — even better than the original,' Edward said, relieved. It was ironic that one of Majuro's environmental problems — garbage on the beach — should come to the rescue of the ecology campaigners.

Senator Jeton Anjain hosted a thank-you dinner; Giff Johnson and Darlene Keju-Johnson threw a farewell party in their home, inviting a group of students to do traditional Marshallese and Gilbertese dances.

'You've disturbed the status quo and we thank you for that,' said Johnson. 'The world has become aware of the plight of the Rongelap people, and the United States Government has been forced to confront the issue.'

Fernando Pereira, Nathalie Mestre, Edward and I visited Majuro township for a parting drink. We met at the seediest and liveliest disco, Smugglers' Cove. It had been given a facelift but it couldn't quite shake off its former image as a pick-up bar when it was the notorious Rainbow Disco. Teenage prostitutes still frequented the place; the rest of the crowd were off-duty policemen, seamen, a pilot and anti-nuclear campaigners.

Steve Sawyer flew to Hawaii before leaving for New Zealand to prepare for the Moruroa campaign. Replacing him was Hans Guyt, the 32-year-old director of Greenpeace Netherlands who also coordinated campaigns against nuclear-waste dumping. It was his first trip to the Pacific although he had already made contact with several Pacific government leaders.

The four-day voyage through the doldrums to Tarawa Atoll in Kiribati left the crew plenty of time to reflect on the Rongelap evacuation and the Kwajalein experience. The exodus seemed to open a whole new chapter for Greenpeace: the importance of humanitarian missions as an integral part of the environment campaigns.

'This dark secret of American nuclear history has been exposed to the rest of the world,' Guyt said. 'The fact that the Rongelap people were forced to leave their home 31 years after being contaminated by fallout is probably the most graphic and tragic statement that can be made about the dangers of nuclear testing and the strongest argument one can make in support of the abolition of nuclear weapons from the face of the earth.'

'When I joined Greenpeace my contribution was to be mainly technical — but the evacuation saw that approach take a back seat,' said Edward. 'We were faced with uprooting a people from their homeland and setting them down on a place which, to them, may as well have been light years away. The first encounter had me scurrying for the engineroom: an old lady on the welcoming launch looking tearfully, forlornly at the island which would have, should have, been her final resting place.

'The farewell on Ebeye really got to me. We ate, we drank, we sang, we danced; they shook our hands, they gave money; I cried.

'How could anyone do to these shy, gentle people what has been done? The only excuse of the guilty was: "It's for the good of mankind".'

Hanne Sorensen, the Danish engineer who surprised Marshall Islanders because they were unused to a woman working in the engineroom, was also fiercely critical.

'The world is too precious to be ruled and ruined by rich, white men with clean hands and sick minds,' she said. 'They claim the Bomb is for our protection yet they test it in other people's land and contaminate other people's children.'

Shipboard life had developed into a smooth, easygoing pattern. The 'Pacific way' had taken over. Skipper Peter Willcox spent some of his spare time on a rowing machine in the converted fish-hold theatre — occasionally watching videos while he rowed. It was a new experience for Willcox who had spent the previous three years commanding the *Warrior* during action-packed campaigns, including the 1983 anti-whaling mission to Siberia.

Willcox was a far more assertive leader than his predecessors, Englishmen Peter Bouquet and Jon Castle. But with the *Rainbow Warrior* now under sail he had to be.

At dawn and dusk, Willcox and radio operator Lloyd Anderson would take star readings with their sextants, even though the ship had satellite navigation. Willcox patiently taught me how to take readings. I took a sun plot and after laboriously working through the mathematical tables managed to fix our position accurately to within two miles.

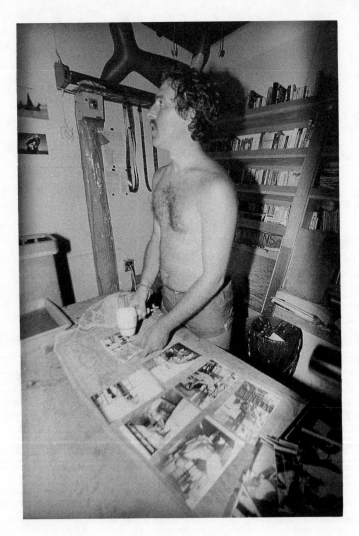

Left: *Fernando Pereira working in the photographic darkroom he rigged up in the ship's library.*

Bunny McDiarmid had been given a saxophone by a friend a year or two before. When things were quiet on deck and nobody was watching a video, she would slip down to the theatre and practise anything from jazz to soul. She didn't like anybody listening — except Fernando Pereira. He had set up a makeshift darkroom in the library next door, with a negative drying bag slung from the ceiling and developing trays on a table among the shelves of more than 500 books. Whenever he heard McDiarmid playing he would stick his head through the door and say: 'Yeah, that's really nice!' He liked jazz, particularly Brazilian and he had a favourite selection on tape.

His charming manner was attractive to women, especially the Marshallese. Nathalie Mestre and he had a little game going between them: they borrowed Marshallese expressions to describe attractive people. *Likatu* — she's gorgeous, *lakatu* — he's desirable, they would say.

Pereira was divorced from his wife Joanne in Amsterdam, but he was devoted to his daughter Marelle, eight, and son Paul, five. In the Marshall Islands he dragged a giant clam shell on deck to scrape down and clean as a souvenir for his family. Although some of his crewmates thought he didn't pull his weight with deck chores, he was a dedicated and hard-working photographer who had a lively sense of humour.

Unused to sea life, something happened to my metabolism and I defected from the vegetarian ranks to become a nocturnal carnivore, a member of the Breakfast Club. It involved a sort of pre-dawn ritual for meat-eaters. The other members were Lloyd Anderson and David Edward. We took it in turns to rise about four o'clock and rustle up breakfast — with liberal dashings of wine, rum, chilli sauce and even vermouth.

A minor split developed between the meat-eaters and vegetarians, provoking annoyed mutterings. But it was finally aired in a deck meeting and resolved. Willcox hardly seemed to eat at all yet he remained extraordinarily healthy.

Finding my below-deck cabin insufferably hot, I had long before taken to sleeping on the boat deck, wrapped in a *pareu*. It was enchanting on moonlit and starry nights, but not when frequent tropical squalls drenched me, or the mizzen sail was dropped.

In their spare time, O'Sullivan and Mestre, who shared a cabin, painted T-shirts and strips of material with brightly coloured designs; engineers Henk Haazen and Edward painted and polished their BMW motorbikes, stored in the carpenter's shop, ready for touring New Zealand; Andy Biedermann and McDiarmid were usually busy on deck, repainting patches where rust showed, completing sail covers and repairing ripped sails.

Every second day, Lloyd Anderson contacted Dick Dillman in San Francisco by radio for news from the movement's offices in 15 countries and other boats in the Greenpeace eco-navy. There were frequent bulletins about the *Fri* on a campaign against industrial pollution in the Great Lakes, the *Vega* arriving in New Zealand to take part in the peace flotilla which would sail to Moruroa, and the *Sirius*.

A message bleeped across the telex from Belgium about the *Sirius*, a 60-metre former Rotterdam pilot vessel: '*Sirius* Confiscated in Antwerp . . . Injunctions from Owners of Dumpship *Wadsy Tanker* and Police.'

The drama had begun just over a month before when the ship left Amsterdam to prevent two Belgian chemical companies from dumping toxic waste in the North Sea. NL Chemicals of Ghent, and Bayer of Antwerp, routinely discharge liquid acids and heavy metals — waste products from titanium dioxide production — into the sea off the Dutch coast.

Five Greenpeace protesters boarded the dumpship *Falco* while leaving Ghent and chained themselves to the discharge pipes, and a waste outlet regulating valve. The ship returned to port, its load untouched. Five days later, the *Sirius* blockaded Antwerp harbour to stop the *Wadsy Tanker* leaving as municipal officials declared support for Greenpeace's attempts to prevent Bayer and NL from dumping toxics. The companies argued they could not afford clean-ups and the campaign ship was impounded. The telex said:

Owners have put a claim of $85,000 on *Sirius* and confiscated ship until claim has been settled. . . . Almost certain Bayer which charters ship is behind this and Greenpeace exposing them . . . meeting unions over action to help release *Sirius* . . . Crew not under arrest and free to move about. Everyone in good spirits, busy making banners for coming court hearing — and playing football.

The *Warrior* crew were glowing, in spite of their sister ship being impounded. 'Bayer are bloody crazy . . . they're just playing into our hands and making things worse for themselves,' Martini Gotje said. 'By taking out an injunction, they've blown up the publicity and public pressure against them over their pollution.'

By mid-June the *Sirius* was the target of two court hearings filed by the owners of the *Wadsy Tanker* and the *Falco* and a Belgian court ordered a ban on Greenpeace blockades in territorial waters and the high seas. The cases could drag on for two years.

Progress toward banning titanium dioxide dumping also drags on. Holland and West Germany, which share the North Sea with Belgium, will outlaw dumping of the chemical — but not until 1989.

Betio, the main *motu* on Tarawa Atoll, is one of the most crowded islands in the Pacific and among the loveliest — despite the rusting remains of four eight-inch guns among the coconut palms and the hulks of about 20 landing craft on the lagoon reef. They bear witness to the four-day battle of Tarawa in 1943, when more than 5,000 Japanese troops and United States marines died.

Memories of the Japanese wartime occupation still linger but now many Kiribati Islanders are worried about Japanese proposals to dump nuclear waste in the Pacific. When the

Rainbow Warrior moored in the lagoon off Betio Island on the morning of 17 June, the first thing mayor Teiraoi Tetebea wanted was an open-air video session about nuclear sea pollution. Tetebea met Hans Guyt and persuaded him to have two public meetings followed by a traditional welcome to the island the next night.

But first there was a brief brush with police. Although the *Rainbow Warrior* was officially visiting Kiribati in support of the country's co-sponsorship with Nauru of a resolution against nuclear waste dumping within the London Dumping Convention, an expatriate police chief decided the ship's crew were troublemakers. He had heard the news on Radio Australia of the protests against the Star Wars programme on Kwajalein and decided the crew were planning something similar in Kiribati.

A couple of policemen were dispatched to escort Guyt, Pereira and Gotje into the Betio police station.

'I'm warning you people you had better not try to protest here — or I'll arrest you,' said the ruddy-faced Englishman. 'This is the Pacific and we don't want meddlers like you around here sowing the seeds of discontent among the islanders.'

Guyt politely pointed out the *Rainbow Warrior* was in Kiribati with the blessing of the Government for a goodwill and educational visit. Why didn't he contact the foreign ministry and find out the facts?

'Well, you stirrers can't just come here and show anything you like to these islanders. They could be misled. It might be subversive.'

Mayor Tetebea arrived, interrupting the police chief. He produced a Government letter welcoming the *Rainbow Warrior* and said the ship's crew were his concern. The group abruptly walked out of the police station.

'Expatriates like that should be sent back home,' growled Guyt. 'Who needs them?'

Islanders packed two thatched-roof *maneaba* (meeting houses) that night for a double screening of the BBC documentary *Commandos of Conservation*, which outlines the history of Greenpeace, and another film about the movement's drive to prevent nuclear waste dumping in the world's oceans.

'The ocean is our birthright for Pacific Islanders,' Tetebea said. 'We need to defend it.' He praised the *Warrior* crew for helping the radiation fallout victims of Rongelap and said he was honoured the ship was visiting Kiribati.

The evening was so successful that the *Rainbow Warrior* crew were embarrassed by the flood of invitations to visit several villages. It was impossible to accept them all in the three-day visit. The next night, the crew were feted by mayor Tetebea and his councillors at a traditional feast followed by *rouia* dancing.

'Maybe we should call ourselves Greenpeace Atoll Cinemas as well as Rainbow Warrior Furniture Removals the evacuation-education-and-entertainment team,' O'Sullivan joked later.

Next day Guyt, Gotje and Pereira met Kiribati's Foreign Secretary and roving ambassador, Atanraoi Baiteke, who Guyt had met at the LDC meeting two years before. Both Kiribati and Nauru had joined the LDC in response to plans by the Japanese Government to dump 10,000 drums of low-level nuclear waste in international waters 600 miles north of the Mariana Islands and a United States Navy scheme to sink at least 100 of its ageing first- and second-generation nuclear submarines in the ocean over the next three decades. Pacific nations had moved to block either plan being implemented. In 1982 the South Pacific Conference adopted the Rarotonga Declaration which urged both Japan and the US to abandon the proposed dumping and research alternative methods of disposal outside the region.

On joining the LDC in 1983, both Nauru and Kiribati had also proposed a ban on all nuclear waste dumping at sea. The proposal had failed to win a two-thirds majority, but a Spanish call for a two-year moratorium on ocean dumping pending a scientific review was adopted.

Now Guyt wanted to find out what Kiribati and Nauru were planning when the moratorium ran out in September. Baiteke assured Guyt there had been no softening of his country's stance and pledged to fight for the dumping ban. (The September 1985 LDC meeting eventually extended indefinitely the nuclear dumping moratorium because of pressure from Pacific nations.)

After discussing the proposed nuclear-free South Pacific zone declaration — later adopted as the historic Rarotonga Treaty in 1985 by the South Pacific Forum — Guyt and his crewmates left.

On the final night in Kiribati, some of the crew were feted at an all-night dance by Betio villagers, and others were treated to a suckling pig and *kikao* (octopus) feast with *tetongo*, fermented coconut milk, on Antenon Island.

Dr Harry Tong, leader of the Opposition Christian Democratic Party, visited for half an hour, and then left, muttering something about Greenpeace members being 'communists'. The *Rainbow Warrior* had arrived in Kiribati in the middle of a domestic crisis about a one-year fisheries treaty with the Soviet fishing agency, Sovrybflot.

President Ieremai Tabai defended his Government's decision to sign the $3 million agreement to grant 16 Soviet ships the right to fish in territorial waters. He ignored claims by the United States that the ships would be more interested in Kwajalein and the American missile tests than fishing.[1]

While Opposition MPs tried to call an emergency session of the *Maneaba ni Maungatabu* (Parliament), islanders from the two northern atolls of Butaritari and Marakei were staging protests — an unusual step in the placid country. One group of village elders who met on Butaritari put up a banner declaring: 'Tabai: Go To Hell With Russian Fishing Rights'.

When I talked to Ambassador Baiteke, he angrily dismissed opposition as being misinformed and said most Kiribati Islanders favoured the agreement.

'They're afraid of a ghost,' he said. 'It's absurd to suggest that Kiribati could turn communist because of a fishing agreement.' He bitterly attacked rumours fed from Australia and the United States that the Russians would build a 'naval base'. 'Such a ridiculous idea was never part of the negotiations. Kiribati is a very pro-West country. The deal

doesn't even allow the Soviet fishermen ashore, except in a real emergency.'

Steve Sawyer was now in Auckland and was preparing for the arrival of the *Rainbow Warrior* in New Zealand. He missed meeting a Frenchwoman called Frederique Bonlieu in the office by about three weeks. Nobody bothered to talk to him much about her; she wasn't all that important then.

The local Greenpeace group originally met in the Ponsonby flat rented by Bette Johnson, mother of Giff Johnson and a livewire organiser who helped plan the 1975 Atom Conference in Suva, Fiji.

One of the founding members was Elaine Shaw. A former nurse, she had been disturbed by terminal cancer cases in a Toronto children's hospital. She returned to New Zealand in 1968 aware of the dangers of nuclear testing but she was far from becoming an activist. One day, with three small children of her own, she was listening to an Auckland radio talkback show appealing for people to help prepare the *Fri* for a world peace odyssey beginning in 1979. She began sorting out provisions — and ended up a member of Greenpeace.

Carol Stewart, a 39-year-old former insurance claims clerk, became involved much later. She wasn't linked with environmental issues at the time and discovered Greenpeace in March 1980 while looking for something different from a conventional nine-to-five job. Within a year her drive and organising abilities won her a fulltime job and by 1984 she was the New Zealand trustee on the Greenpeace Council in Lewes.

For years Elaine Shaw had been coping with a problem Greenpeace has in the Pacific. Greenpeace is careful to avoid being involved in partisan politics but in the Pacific it is almost impossible to separate an issue such as nuclear testing from political independence. The experience of countries like the Micronesian republic of Belau, which adopted the world's first nuclear-free constitution in 1979, and Vanuatu, which became independent from Britain and France in 1980, show this. Vanuatu has championed a nuclear-free Pacific and other independence movements in the region, from the Kanaks in New Caledonia to Tahiti to Irian Jaya. Unlike other Pacific countries which gained independence peacefully, Vanuatu survived the violence of an attempted secession, encouraged by American business interests and France. Pacific leaders such as Prime Minister Walter Lini of Vanuatu squarely blame the nuclear oppression of the region on colonialism.

At grassroots level the link is perhaps even stronger. The nuclear-free movement was reformed in a 1980 conference in Hawaii as the Nuclear-Free and Independent Pacific Movement. At the following NFIP conference in Port Vila during 1983, a People's Charter was reaffirmed which declared:

We, the people of the Pacific, are rapidly regaining control of our lands, and the fact that we have inherited the basic administration system imposed upon us by alien imperialistic and colonial powers does not imply that we have to perpetuate them and the preferential racist policies that went with them.

The people of the Pacific have been victimised too long by foreign powers. The Western imperialistic and colonial powers invaded our defenceless region; they took over our lands and subjugated our people to their whims. This form of alien colonial, political and military domination unfortunately persists as an evil cancer in some of our native territories such as Tahiti, New Caledonia, Aotearoa [New Zealand] and Australia.

Our environment continues to be despoiled by foreign powers developing nuclear weapons for a strategy of warfare that has no winners, no liberators and imperils the survival of all humankind . . .

The charter calls on all governments of the Pacific to prevent all tests of nuclear explosive devices — including those described as 'peaceful'; all nuclear test facilities; all tests of nuclear weapon delivery vehicles and systems; all storage, transit, deployment or any other form of presence of nuclear weapons on land or on board ships, submarines and aircraft within the zone; all bases assisting any nuclear weapons delivery system; all transit, storage, release or dumping of radioactive material; and uranium mining, processing and transport. It also asks governments to withdraw from all mutual defence alliances with nuclear powers.

As Greenpeace's coordinator on nuclear issues in New Zealand, Elaine Shaw first made links with Vanuatu in 1978

when she met Hilda Lini and Donald Kalpokas. Lini, sister of Father Walter Lini, was then editor of the pro-independence Vanuaaku Party newspaper *Viewpoints*, and Kalpokas was a key party leader who became Education Minister after independence. [2] Shaw first met Walter Lini on a marae in Mangere the following year and she took him to Bastion Point where Maori land rights activists were camped. They were demanding that the Government hand the land back to tribal ownership. Lini had close ties with New Zealand having been educated as an Anglican priest at St John's Theological College in Auckland.

In the years that followed the Vanuatu Government and Greenpeace developed informal links through Shaw. Vanuatu saw Greenpeace as an ally against continued French nuclear testing; Shaw regarded Port Vila as a uniquely sympathetic government.

When Prime Minister Lini visited the Greenpeace office in Auckland during December 1984, Shaw asked if his Government would welcome the *Rainbow Warrior*.

'We would be honoured to receive her,' Lini replied.

Sawyer's first contact with Vanuatu from Auckland was also warm. Clarence Marae, second secretary in the Foreign Ministry, had just sent a telex message. It ended: 'Peace and Solidarity'.

'Encouraging', thought Sawyer. How often did Greenpeace get a note like that from a government?

Left: *Father Walter Lini, Prime Minister of Vanuatu, an ardent supporter of Greenpeace's aspirations in the Pacific.*

Past the stark rocky outcrop of Devil's Point, across the open stretch of sea in Mele Bay, sailed the *Rainbow Warrior*. It was 27 June and there was a rendezvous to keep. The telex had been busy with messages from Marae. It was clear a red carpet welcome was being planned in Vanuatu.

At 9 a.m. the radio crackled. 'Good morning, *Rainbow Warrior*, we can see you now,' said the Port Vila pilot station. 'A welcome flotilla is on its way to escort you in.'

At the entrance to Port Vila harbour the *Warrior* was met by a small fleet of about 10 boats, including Government launches, speedboats, yachts and an outrigger canoe flying peace and nuclear-free flags. Horns tooted and schoolchildren on one of the launches cheered.

Peter Willcox watched them coming through binoculars. 'Hell, they're all dressed up,' he said. The crew scrambled out of work clothes and smartened themselves up.

Two launches came alongside. The first person to leap on board was Tahitian independence leader Tetua Mai, flamboyant president of the self-styled Maohi provisional government. Mai, who had been jailed three years before when French authorities suppressed his Maohi Party, handed out shell leis.[3] He was joined by other Tahitian independence leaders. They had been invited to the annual congress of the Vanuaaku Party on Tanna Island the following week. Vanuatu radio and press journalists also came aboard and made a live broadcast from the deck.

The Government launch *Euphrosyne*, the former British Resident Commissioner's touring vessel, drew alongside and Prime Minister Walter Lini, Foreign Minister Sela Molisa and several other cabinet ministers climbed on board. Coordinator Hans Guyt hobbled around. A few days earlier he had sliced his foot on the giant clamshell Pereira had brought on board and it had swelled up like a balloon. I propped him up on a stool for his interviews.

Lini and his entourage returned to the *Euphrosyne*, along with most of the *Warrior's* crew, to be taken to a welcome by the city of Port Vila. The waterfront park was lined with more than 3,000 Vanuatu people and a banner which said: 'Nuclear-Free Port Vila Welcomes Rainbow Warrior'.

'You are like gladiators of the ocean,' said mayor Serge Puyo-Festa, a French businessman, presenting a bronze freedom-of-the-city medallion from Port Vila to skipper Willcox. Tahitian women living in Vila garlanded the crew with hibiscus leis.

The *Vanuatu Weekly*, the country's trilingual newspaper, announced news of the ship's arrival under a tongue-twisting headline in Bislama, the pidgin language:

> RENBOU WORIA SIP BLONG KRIN
> PIS WE I AGENSEM OL NIUKLEA
> AKTIVITI PAS TRU LONG VANUATU
> RERE BLONG GO FROM MORUROA

Loosely translated, it said: '*Rainbow Warrior* calls on Vanuatu before her peaceful assault on Moruroa and possibly the French Navy's might!'

After Guyt, Willcox, McDiarmid and Biedermann met Lini and Molisa the next day for talks about nuclear testing and the LDC issue, the prime minister hosted a cocktail party at Port Vila's Besa Club in honour of the *Warrior*.

'Colonialism and nuclearism in the Pacific are part of the same evil,' Lini said. 'To eradicate this evil from our region we have to deal with it from its root — colonialism. Nuclear testing will continue for as long as colonialism remains and nuclear powers exploit Pacific people to play with their deadly weapons.'

Lini told how in February 1982 the Vanuatu Government had given a lead to Pacific countries by prohibiting two American warships from visiting Port Vila because Washington would not give assurance that nuclear devices were not being carried on board.

The prime minister warned the *Rainbow Warrior* crew they faced danger at the hands of the French Navy. He told them they had the support of Vanuatu.

Martini Gotje replied: 'For too long people in the Pacific have paid with their health and in many cases their lives, with their land and their future for the "security" of superpowers and those countries that aspire to be one,' he said. 'In our fight to prevent nuclear war it is our duty to be in solidarity with those for whom nuclear war has already begun a long time ago . . .

Gotje spoke from the heart but he had shared a bottle of vodka with some Vanuatu friends earlier in the afternoon and as he became more passionate, expletives began punctuating his speech. When he paused for breath, Lloyd Anderson began clapping and the rest of the crew quickly joined in.

In spite of the rain which lasted four days, the ship was made 'open house' during the weekend and hundreds of people visited.

Grace Molisa, wife of the Foreign Minister and second secretary in the Prime Minister's Office, gave me a collection of her poetry, *Black Stone*. It is dedicated to the independence struggle and women's rights.

> *Neo-colonialism*
> *witlessly*
> *playing*
> *into the hands*
> *of Foreign sharks*
> *ready*
> *to swallow up*
> *unsuspecting prey.*

Charles Rara, 29, a newly appointed research officer in the Prime Minister's Office, was chosen to join the *Warrior* as the ni-Vanuatu representative on the voyage to Moruroa. One of the founders of the anti-nuclear Vanuatu Social Concerns Committee, he got on well with the rest of the crew.

Rara was issued with a diplomatic passport to protect him and to make things as awkward as possible for French authorities.

The night before we left Vanuatu, Rara asked Guyt, Gotje and myself to come to a farewell *kava*-drinking

Right: Warrior *crew going ashore at Port Vila for a mayoral welcome.*

ceremony organised by his family on the outskirts of Port Vila.

Kava grounds are usually sacred and are traditionally male retreats. Sometimes called 'native beer', *kava* is made from the *Piper methysticum*, a shrub in the pepper family. The roots are pounded into a paste and added to water and the drink has the effect of gradually paralysing the body.

I warned Guyt and Gotje of the effects, but they didn't seem to believe me.

'I don't feel a bloody thing,' said Gotje after the first bowl. Three hours later, when it was time to leave, we could barely move. Our minds were perfectly clear, but our bodies from the chest down felt glued to the ground. Gotje, taller than both of us, was helped to his feet by three men.

We arrived back at the ship walking stiffly like wooden toys. We had thought of taking some *kava* with us and perhaps anticipating this Rara brought a sackful with him on board. But a gale after leaving port on 1 July soaked the roots with sea water, perhaps mercifully ruining the stuff.

For three days the storm raged, keeping us below decks. Spirits sagged. Radio Australia broadcast the news of the assassination of Belau President Haruo Remeliik. The report said:

> The president of the western Pacific island republic of Belau has been shot and killed. A Government spokesman said that Haruo Remeliik had been shot about three times after getting out of his car at his home in the capital, Koror. The presidential press secretary said Mr Remeliik had returned home from a fishing trip with friends and he was alone at the time of the shooting. He said he could not comment on the motive for the killing.

Remeliik, 51, was a staunch advocate of the nuclear-free constitution when it was first adopted. He had been under increasing pressure from the United States to revoke the nuclear-free clause of the constitution in exchange for the Compact of Free Association. Three plebiscites have failed to change the clause. (In September 1981 his house was bombed during a strike by civil servants.)

Good news was relayed from San Francisco about the daring night escape of the *Sirius*. Defying the Belgian injunction, the crew cut the docking chains and sliced off the upper half of the masts so the ship could sneak under several low bridges and slip down the Schelde-Rhine canal safely across the Dutch border.

The weather cleared before the *Warrior* reached New Zealand's North Cape. The sun shone weakly; the heat of the Pacific was now behind us. Pereira talked to Biedermann about going together on a ski trip to Mount Ruapehu when the ship docked in New Zealand after he had bought Christmas presents for his two children.

On Sunday, 7 July, a fleet of small boats welcomed the *Rainbow Warrior* into Auckland harbour. It was Bunny McDiarmid's first time back for almost seven years.

As the crew and well-wishers celebrated that night, they did not know of a curious discovery on the other side of downtown Auckland. A few nights before the *Warrior* berthed at Marsden Wharf, a waiter in the Last and First Café had found a crumpled piece of paper on a table. It said: 'Beware Greenpeace. There's a traitor in your midst — we'll do you!'

Below the words, a crude sketch showed a ship at the bottom of the sea.

Footnotes to Chapter Six

1. Kiribati, formerly the British-ruled Gilbert Islands, is a country of only 60,000 people spread over 33 islands and atolls. Nevertheless, it claims a vast exclusive economic zone covering five million square kilometres of the central Pacific. It regards tuna fish as its only resource. However, American fishing trawlers have stirred resentment among small Pacific nations because they continually ignore the 200-mile economic zones. The fishing agreement between Kiribati and the Soviet Union would probably never have been signed but for unhappiness over American attitudes.

2. Before 1979 the mainly anglophone Vanuaaku Pati (Our People) was called the National Party. It set up a provisional government in the Anglo-French condominium of the New Hebrides under Walter Lini's leadership. Subsequently, it won a sweeping electoral victory and on 30 July 1980 led the country to independence as Vanuatu (Our Land). The opposition Union of Moderate Parties (UPM) is also committed to nuclear-free policies but does not support independence movements in French territories.

3. *Maohi*, the language of Tahitians, is similar to Maori in the Cook Islands and New Zealand. Now the term is being used frequently to identify political groups opposed to French control.

CHAPTER SEVEN

The Death of a Warrior

The French may be able to sink the Rainbow Warrior *but what they, and the other nuclear powers, need to realise is that they cannot sink the rainbow.*
— Greenpeace campaigner Gerd Leipold

PIHA BEACH on Auckland's lonely west coast was wild, bitterly cold and rainswept. Huddled around a one-bar heater in a backroom of the two-storeyed surf club were several Greenpeace officials trying to keep warm. It was early on the morning of 11 July. In a few hours a three-day meeting of the Australian, Canadian, New Zealand and United States branches of the movement was due to start. Jim Bohlen, an American composite-materials researcher who had once worked with Buckminster Fuller, and biologist Dr Patrick Moore had flown in from Canada the previous afternoon. The pair crewed on the *Phyllis Cormack* in the original Greenpeace mission to Amchitka in 1971. They had driven out to Piha with New Zealand national coordinator Carol Stewart, Australian Mike Bossley and and Claire Gerson, cook on the *Vega*.

An exhausted Steve Sawyer and Kelly Rigg, who ran the endangered wildlife campaign in the United States, had arrived about midnight with Australian Michelle Sheather from the *Rainbow Warrior*. Elaine Shaw brought them out, stopped for a quick beer and then drove home to Titirangi.

Now Sawyer was sharing the remnants of a bottle of Captain Morgan rum, given to him as a present for his twenty-ninth birthday. It was late and he wanted to get some sleep. Everybody thought it was time to turn in.

The telephone rang. Caretaker Robyn Mercer picked up the phone in a room at the other end of the surf club and called Sawyer.

Who the hell could be ringing me at this time of the morning, grumbled Sawyer to himself. He looked at his watch: it was 1.07 a.m. A distraught Elaine Shaw was on the line.

'Elaine, what's wrong?'

'Come quickly, Steve. It's the *Rainbow Warrior*. There's been an explosion on board. She's sunk at the dock!'

'Stop joking, Elaine. What do you mean? What are you talking about?'

Sawyer couldn't believe her words and Shaw said them again, slowly, letting them sink in. But Sawyer was so stunned he didn't hear Shaw add that one, perhaps two, people were missing.

Sawyer ran down the hallway, blurting out the shocking news. An explosion on board, but he didn't know any more. (He didn't realise until later that it was the second birthday shock on the voyage.)

Carol Stewart called the police. All they told her was that something had happened and it would be wise to return to Auckland immediately. Michelle Sheather, who hadn't driven around Auckland before, grabbed the keys to the car. She drove Sawyer, Rigg and Stewart in a madcap 40-minute sprint, dodging opossums along the windy road.

From Titirangi, Shaw was also heading for Marsden Wharf, 20 minutes away. She had only just got home after dropping the others off at Piha when a *New Zealand Herald* reporter was on the phone: 'I'd like to talk about the *Rainbow Warrior . . .'*

'Well, that's a bit strange at one o'clock in the morning,' she snapped.

'Oh, I'm sorry,' said the reporter. 'Didn't you know? Your ship's been sunk. There were two explosions and one, possibly two, people are missing.'

Shaw slammed the phone down, shocked. It couldn't be true.

The phone rang again. This time it was a local radio station.

'No, I don't know anything about it,' she yelled into the phone and hung up.

She rang the surf club at Piha and as she waited for Sawyer to come to the phone, she felt stupid. She wasn't absolutely sure it was true.

But when she reached the gates of Marsden Wharf she saw policemen guarding the entrance and beyond them she could see the partly sunken *Warrior*, leaning at a 45 degree angle against the concrete dock.

Shaw felt ill and drove down Quay Street to the wharf police station where the crew were. Her years of hard work to get the *Rainbow Warrior* to New Zealand to lead a protest to Moruroa had been destroyed — three days after the ship had arrived.

The evening of Wednesday, 10 July had begun noisily: Steve Sawyer, Elaine Shaw, Carol Stewart and a few other Greenpeace members met Pat Moore, Jim Bohlen, Mike Bossley and Michelle Sheather to celebrate Sawyer's birthday. They gathered in the Mexican Café in Auckland's Albert Street at about six p.m. for an 'el cheapo' dinner of enchiladas and tortillas.

Sawyer left just before eight to go to the *Rainbow Warrior* for a meeting with the skippers of the fleet going to Moruroa — *Alliance, Django, Kliss II, Varangian,* and *Vega*. They hadn't had a chance to meet together before.

'Happy birthday, Steve,' said Margaret Mills, the sprightly 55-year-old relief cook from Waiheke Island. She was taking Nathalie Mestre's place who was staying at her island retreat for a break. Mills had prepared sweet corn fritters with red and green peppers, baked potatoes in sour cream and brussels sprouts for the crew's dinner. For Sawyer, she made a chocolate cake decorated with a jelly bean rainbow and three candles for his 29 years.

Sawyer sat at the head of the table in the messroom. Everybody was tucking into the birthday cake or sipping wine left over from a party the night before. There had been more than 30 people of many nationalities milling around.

Sawyer noticed Dutch campaigner Rein Achterberg, now resident in New Zealand and the one responsible for coordinating the peace flotilla. He was talking to a stranger at the other end of the mess. The stranger looked to be in his mid-20s and more like a bank clerk than a Greenpeace member.

Earlier, Achterberg had seen the young man wandering around and invited him on board. Visitors to the *Rainbow Warrior* were common, but there was something unusual about this man. It wasn't that he was French — Greenpeace counts many French nationals among its supporters. Achterberg gave the man a slice of birthday cake and asked him what his interest was in Greenpeace. He said his name was François Verlet and he was a pacifist. Yet he was vague about any connections with a French peace group. Verlet said he was travelling to Tahiti that night. Could he perhaps help from Papeete?

'How?' he was asked.

'I've heard you're planning to send some canoes from the southern Polynesian atolls to Moruroa,' Verlet said. 'Perhaps I could help organise this through my friends in Tahiti.'

Achterberg thought it was strange Verlet should say this. It was true that several ideas had been discussed with some anti-nuclear Tahitian activists but they had been shelved when David McTaggart had ordered that the 12-mile territorial limit around Moruroa was not to be breached. Greenpeace is an open organisation but it was curious this man knew anything about such an obscure idea.

Verlet's presence just six weeks after another stranger from France, Frederique Bonlieu, had been working in the Greenpeace office made Achterberg rather suspicious.

As Verlet left he said to Sawyer: 'Happy birthday! I hope you make it to Moruroa.'

It was almost 8.15 p.m. Most of the 14 people attending the meeting were in the theatre, forward of the engineroom. Sawyer climbed down the ladder through the carpenter's shop to join them. Skippers Tony Still (*Alliance*), Russ Munro (*Django*), Richard Rae (*Kliss II*), Alistair Robinson (*Varangian*) and veteran campaigner Chris Robinson, bound for Moruroa on his third voyage in the *Vega*, were all there. From the *Warrior* were Willcox, Gotje, Hoffmann and Anderson, who had been to Moruroa in 1981 on board the *Vega*.

They poured over the charts, discussed possible rendezvous points, safety, a schedule for leaving Auckland and other practicalities. There was a lot of joking and laughter.

Elaine Shaw drove down to the wharf after leaving the Mexican Café. She then went to Herne Bay, a few minutes away, to pick up a wok and other cooking gear for the Piha meeting. When she came back, the meeting was still going, so she took Australian council members Mike Bossley and Michelle Sheather on tours of the *Rainbow Warrior*

— separately. Both times she went through the engineroom and couldn't see anything unusual.

Russ Munro, whose sloop *Django* was moored on the portside of the *Warrior*, noticed something strange bobbing in the water and went in a boat to investigate. It was a floating bag of brussels sprouts.

It was now 9.30 p.m. A couple of yachtsmen vigilantes were drinking coffee and keeping an eye on the waterfront at Hobson Bay. Members of the Auckland Outboard Boating Club on Tamaki Drive, they were keeping watch for thieves who had been stealing from the boats. One nudged the other. Coming ashore, with its engine cut, was a grey-and-black inflatable speedboat. It looked like a French-made Zodiac, which were rare in New Zealand. They watched carefully. A man on board was dressed in a wet suit and a red woollen hat. After dumping a Yamaha engine in the sea under Ngapipi Bridge the man beached the inflatable and was picked up by a Toyota Hi-ace campervan along Tamaki Drive. In the van were a man and a woman.

The Zodiac had just come from the *Rainbow Warrior*. Two frogmen, using rebreather scuba gear which didn't release tell-tale bubbles, had planted two limpet mines below the waterline on the ship's hull timed to explode 10 minutes before midnight. The larger one, about 20 kilos of explosives, was clamped to the engineroom and the other at the stern, where it would cripple the steering gear. Both bombs were on the starboard side, next to the wharf.

After planting the bombs, the frogmen had parted and the man in the red hat had gone ashore at Hobson Bay for his rendezvous with the van. Driving away, the three people thought the operation had gone smoothly. In less than three hours the *Warrior* would cease to be a problem for France.

They hadn't reckoned on being spotted by the vigilantes. One of them wrote down the licence plate number, LB8945. Later, the New Zealand police would identify the couple in the van as French secret service agents Major Alain Mafart and Captain Dominique Prieur. The other man was Chief Petty Officer Jean-Michel Barcelo, another spy.

On board the *Warrior* the meeting in the theatre was dragging on. It was almost 11 p.m. when Kelly Rigg poked her head through the door and said, 'Come on you guys. Don't take all night. We've got to get to Piha.'

Within a few minutes the meeting ended. Sawyer left for Piha. Some of the others wandered into the messroom and poured themselves a drink. Lloyd Anderson went to the radio room to read on his bunk. He fell asleep with his lamp on. Margaret Mills also went to bed, in my old lower-deck cabin, about 11.30 and went to sleep almost immediately. Edward, Pereira, Gotje, Achterberg and some of the others stayed in the mess chatting over a drink.

CRUMPPPPPPPP! Edward was hurled off his chair as the 418-tonne ship shuddered with a massive explosion. Others were thrown against the wall.

'Bloody hell . . . It's from the engineroom,' Edward shouted, as the lights plunged off and then on again. He glanced at the brass messroom clock before the lights flickered out altogether. It read 11.49. Everybody was trying to get out of the messroom. Edward wrenched open the engineroom door and couldn't believe his eyes. The sea was pouring in and had already filled two-thirds of the engineroom. As it swirled through the seared metal from the hole Edward couldn't see, the water hissed like a gigantic steam bath.

Willcox, asleep in his cabin, woke up instantly. It seemed as if something had rammed the *Warrior*. He scrambled out of bed near-naked and raced down the passageway to join Edward at the engineroom. One look was enough.

'Abandon ship,' he yelled. 'Everybody get the hell out of here!'

Anderson had never felt or heard anything like this explosion before. He stuck his head out on the bridge. Then he grabbed his trousers and shoes. By the time he had walked across the bridge, he could hear Willcox yelling and water was already pouring over the main deck.

Mills woke with a jolt. She thought there had been two explosions. Immediately before the engineroom blast, somebody had dropped the gangway on deck. She could hear water gushing into the ship. It sounded like somebody had left the firehose cock running. In spite of having no lightbulb in the cabin, Mills managed to pull on her tracksuit and sneakers. But she couldn't find her glasses. She couldn't see her way around without them. Biedermann, the ship's doctor, appeared in the cabin doorway and grabbed her.

'I've got to find my glasses,' Mills pleaded.

'Don't be silly, Margaret,' he said. 'You can't . . . The ship's sinking.' Biedermann half pulled her up on deck and then on to the wharf. Mills had had little experience with boats — apart from protesting against the United States nuclear submarine *Haddo* her boating experience had been limited to the Waiheke ferries.

Terisa Tutte, asleep on board the *Django*, awoke with the bang. She leapt up on deck to see people scrambling across the flagship as she listed towards the wharf. 'Where's Margaret?' called a voice in the darkness. But a moment later she saw her friend Mills appear on deck.

Then came another huge explosion. Tutte saw an electric blue flash underwater at the stern. The sea bubbled.

Russ Munro jumped on board the *Django*. 'The bastards are for real. Let's get out of here,' he said. They slipped the moorings, drifted out into the harbour and used a spinnaker pole to sail around to nearby Princes Wharf.

Everything was chaotic on Marsden Wharf. Shouts and curses were coming from all directions.

'Look out, the mast is coming down!' somebody yelled as the ship slowly heeled over towards the wharf. Pereira was worried about his cameras, down in his cabin behind the engineroom. He shouted to other crew he was going below. Gotje said he was going down, too. He couldn't find Hanne Sorensen. Maybe she was still in her cabin.

Right: *The* Rainbow Warrior *at Marsden Wharf after the bombing.* (Gil Hanly)

Gotje and Pereira scrambled down to the bottom of the stairs together. It took Gotje only a second to see Sorensen wasn't in the cabin and he dashed back up the steps. But Pereira was trapped in his cabin when the second blast came almost directly below, about two minutes after the first explosion.

Willcox and Edward were in a panic. Gotje had got back on the wharf, but there was no sign of Pereira. They quickly did a head count. 'Where's Hanne?' moaned Gotje. Somebody was sure she had gone for a walk before the blasts. It seemed only Pereira was definitely missing. Willcox and Edward climbed on to the top of the wheelhouse and wrenched aside the steel flap over the smokestack. But peering down at the submerged engineroom they realised their efforts were futile. It was a job for divers.

Steve Sawyer and the others had arrived from Piha. They tried to get on the dock, but were directed to the wharf police station where they found the crew, ashen-faced. Some were wrapped in blankets.

As they entered the foyer just after 2 a.m., Hans Guyt was leaning against the door. 'They blew up the boat and they've killed Fernando,' he moaned. Guyt was one of Pereira's closest friends.

Left: *The submerged deck of the* Rainbow Warrior *(Gil Hanly)*

Right: *Shattered washbasins in the heads of the* Rainbow Warrior. *The damage was caused by the second bomb, almost directly below the heads area.* (Gil Hanly)

'We've lost the *Warrior*,' said Chris Robinson, who had worked like a slave in the London docks seven years earlier to prepare the ship as a campaign vessel. Fears about Hanne Sorensen were over; she had turned up after a walk in the city.

Willcox told Sawyer the cause of the explosions could not be identified. The only dangerous substances stored on the ship were 14 fuel drums on the main deck and a couple of oxyacetylene cylinders in the forecastle. Both were well forward of the blasts. Most of the fuel drums, used for supplying the outboard motors, were empty and had been filled with seawater for safety.

Static electricity was sometimes a risk when a ship's fuel tanks were being cleaned out. But that was rare. These were big explosions with no smoke or fire. The ship had sunk in three minutes. A bizarre accident — or sabotage!

'It has to be bombs — we've been bombed,' Willcox said. Chief engineer Edward sat silently in a corner. He knew his engineroom had been immaculate. He knew it couldn't have been his fault. But was there something he had overlooked? Surely, nobody would bomb a peace ship. He remained quiet for the rest of the day, intently listening to radio news broadcasts, waiting for evidence that it had nothing to do with the engineroom.

A French connection seemed obvious — the *Warrior* had been bound for Moruroa. But the United States had been embarrassed by the evacuation from Rongelap. Could the CIA have done it? Or was it right-wing extremists from New Caledonia? The ship wasn't only challenging French nuclear tests; it had a ni-Vanuatu national on board and Vanuatu was the strongest Pacific supporter of the Kanak struggle for independence. Noumea had become a haven for racist mercenaries since Algeria became independent in 1962.

At Piha, Pat Moore managed to squeeze more information out of the police and he phoned David McTaggart in Britain. McTaggart was with Monika Griefahn and Peter Wilkinson, two other board members, at Bournemouth for the International Whaling Commission meeting. It was agreed Moore would handle the news media, Sawyer the ship liaison and McTaggart would tap his international contacts for a 'deep throat'. Within five days McTaggart knew the sabotage had been ordered at the highest levels of the French Government.

The Greenpeace office in Auckland was a madhouse. So was the international headquarters in Lewes, Sussex. New Zealander Roger Wilson, coordinator of the Antarctic campaign, took charge of communications. A telex message chattered to the rest of the movement's 15 member countries:

ATTN: GREENPEACE, ALL OFFICES
10 JULY 1985
FROM: GREENPEACE INTERNATIONAL
URGENT . . . URGENT . . . URGENT . . .
APPROX TWO HOURS AGO, RAINBOW WARRIOR SUNK BY TWO EXPLOSIONS IN AUCKLAND HARBOUR, NEW ZEALAND. SABOTAGE SUSPECTED. VERY LITTLE NEWS FORTHCOMING

Right: *As this diagram shows, the mines were so placed to maximise damage to the* Warrior.

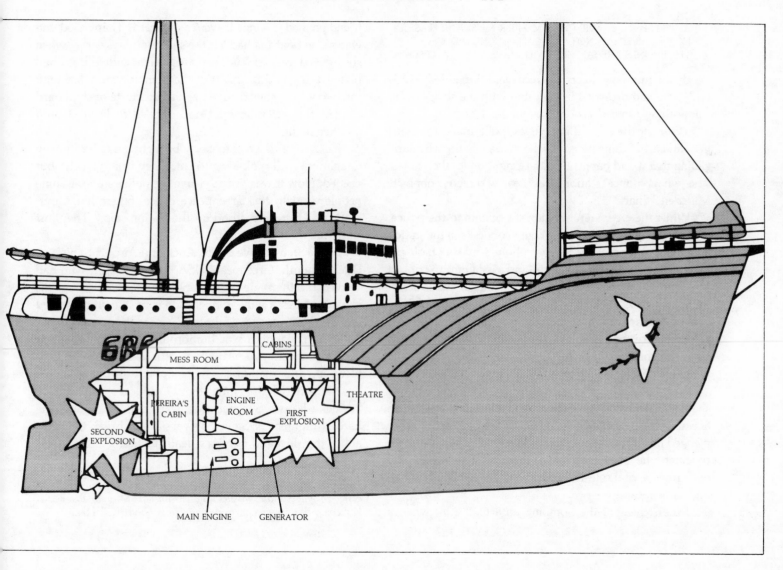

SECOND EXPLOSION

PEREIRA'S CABIN

MESS ROOM

CABINS

ENGINE ROOM

FIRST EXPLOSION

THEATRE

MAIN ENGINE

GENERATOR

AT PRESENT . . . ONE CREW MEMBER MISSING. PLEASE DO NOT . . . REPEAT NOT . . . CALL AUCKLAND OFFICE . . . TELEPHONES ARE JAMMED. WILL HAVE MORE INFO SOON.

By 4 a.m., navy divers had recovered Fernando Pereira's body. He had drowned in his cabin with the straps to his camera bag tangled around one of his legs.

'We'll get them,' said one young policeman. 'We don't like this sort of thing here.' For the police it was particularly galling that it had happened almost right under their noses. The wharf police station was nearly directly opposite Marsden Wharf.

While the crew were making statements to the police, Guyt and Sawyer took over a couple of desks in the station and made phone calls. Sawyer phoned marine biologist Mike Donoghue in Coromandel and asked him to contact MP Fran Wilde. She had arranged a tour of the *Warrior* by fellow backbench MPs Richard Northey, Eddie Isbey, Trevor Mallard and Judy Keall on the Monday night, two nights before the bombing. They had discussed possible Government assistance for the peace flotilla. Donoghue waited until almost seven a.m. to phone Wilde.

'Yes, I know . . . I heard it on the six o'clock news,' she said. 'I'm utterly appalled. And of course it's not an accident. I knew it was fishy as soon as I heard it.' She pledged the Government would do everything in its power to catch the culprits. During the next few weeks she performed a vital role as a go-between for the Government and Greenpeace.

I didn't hear of the bombing until 6.30 a.m. when a friend phoned, saying, 'Haven't you heard? Thank God you weren't on board'. I had left the ship four days earlier when she arrived in Auckland, my assignment ended. But I had planned to spend the night of the bombing on board with my two young sons to give them a brief taste of shipboard life. At the last moment I had decided to leave it until another night.

Just before dawn somebody brought a batch of gooey doughnuts with pink icing to eat. They were ghastly, but needed. Now it was time to leave the police station. Some people went to the Greenpeace office, others like Guyt, Gotje and Sorensen stood on the station steps. They just stared at the lifeless ship.

Elaine Shaw drove out to Auckland Airport to pick up Peter Bahouth, Greenpeace USA board director, who had arrived for the regional meeting. When he filled out his contact address on the immigration card, the official noted the word Greenpeace and said, 'A pity about your boat.'

'What?' Bahouth was dumbfounded.

'Oh, haven't you heard?' the official said. 'It's sunk — blew up, or something!'

Nathalie Mestre rang the Greenpeace office from Waiheke Island. She had not heard a thing. It was the hardest moment of Steve Sawyer's life to break the news about the ship and Pereira's death to her.

Right: *The morning after the bombing in the Greenpeace office in Nagel House, Auckland. From left: Skipper Peter Willcox , Bunny McDiarmid, and Hans Guyt.* (Gil Hanly)

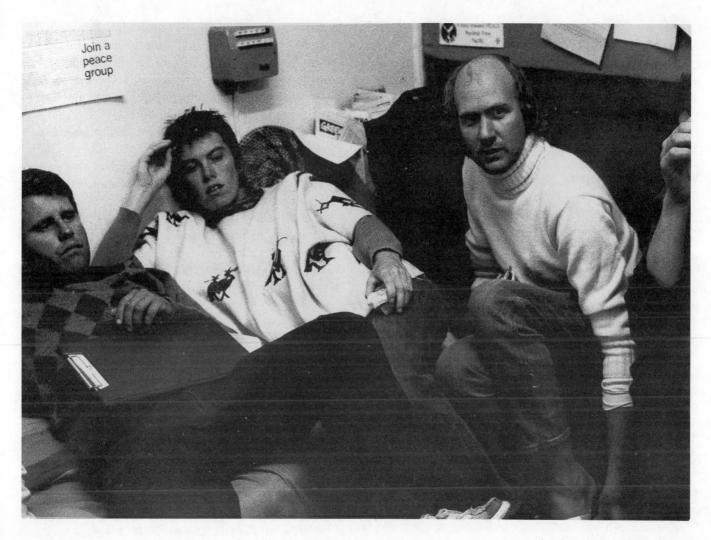

Grace O'Sullivan needed to be told, too. She was relief crew on the scow *Te Aroha*, returning from Great Barrier Island. Bene Hoffmann was in Taupo. Henk Haazen and Bunny McDiarmid were staying at her parents' place in Herne Bay.

Margaret Mills wrote an untitled poem dedicated to the memory of Fernando Pereira. She had known him for just three days.

> *No martyr he*
> *seeking death between the narrow walls*
> *of man-made faith,*
> *He gave his work and enjoyed the giving.*
> *He should be famed not for dying*
> *but for living.*
> *For how he used his life*
> *and for caring.*
> *He did not give his life,*
> *they took it.*
> *He left a memory of life and laughter.*

In the Marshall Islands, the Rongelap Islanders were shocked. When Senator Jeton Anjain heard the news, he said, 'What have they done to *our* boat?' Giff Johnson and Darlene Keju-Johnson sent a heart-tugging message to Greenpeace.

Philippe Chatenay and Walter Guerin, two of the journalists on board the *Warrior* for the Rongelap evacuation, sent a telex from Paris saying: 'We are sad . . . sad for humanity. You give your time, your life to save, preserve what you can in our crazy world. We're wondering if your fight still has meaning. Must you give so much to people who want to hear nothing?'

From Port Vila, Prime Minister Walter Lini phoned Greenpeace to express his outrage and to reassure Charles Rara of the Vanuatu people's support. Rara was sharing Pereira's cabin but had gone ashore to stay with friends earlier in the evening.

'I'm not scared by the bombing and I'm still keen to go to Moruroa,' he said defiantly.

'We cannot allow Fernando Pereira to die in vain,' Pat Moore said. A telephone conference between the five world directors decided the peace flotilla must still go to Moruroa.

Later divers discovered a hole about two metres by three metres blown inwards on the starboard side of the ship's engineroom. Later, they found a second badly damaged area around the propeller shaft.

'Sabotage, says Greenpeace,' read the banner headline in that afternoon's *Auckland Star*, but the *New Zealand Herald* was even more blunt: 'Terrorism Strikes'.

Davey Edward was relieved.

CHAPTER EIGHT

Blunderwatergate

I want to return to the outrage against the Rainbow
Warrior . . . *our condemnation . . . is an absolute
condemnation against a criminal act. The guilty, whoever
they be, have to pay for this crime.*
— French Prime Minister Laurent Fabius

FREDERIQUE BONLIEU came to Greenpeace New Zealand warmly recommended. Jean-Marie Vidal, a French contact of Elaine Shaw, had written to her to say Bonlieu was coming to New Zealand. Shaw had been in touch with Vidal since the 1975 Atom conference in Suva, Fiji. Now he was director of a nautical school in Port Carmague, west of Marseilles.

'Very soon one of my friends, Frederique Bonlieu, is coming to New Zealand,' Vidal wrote on 3 April 1985. 'She's a young woman who is coming to your country to study geography. She is a scientist, excellent sailor and shares our beliefs. Help her and share your views and actions with her.'

Vidal suggested she could gather information on South Pacific people and politics and write some articles for French newspapers. The French were beginning to understand the Kanak struggle for independence in New Caledonia and its implications for French Polynesia.

'And then when will the Mediterranean become nuclear-free?' he wrote.

Three weeks later, on 22 April, Bonlieu arrived unannounced in Auckland. She stayed the night in a city youth hostel, less than 200 metres from the Greenpeace office in Nagel House. The next day she phoned Greenpeace and arranged to meet Shaw outside the chief post office.

Bonlieu was a stocky blonde with fine-boned features, pale skin and short-cropped hair. But what struck Shaw the most was her style of dress. Bonlieu wore jeans and a sweat shirt — navy and white, with a red scarf around her neck. Blue, white and red, the colours of the *Tricolore*, were what she wore most of the time she was in New Zealand.

'You're looking very patriotic,' Shaw told her.

Shaw had no way of guessing just how 'patriotic' the woman really was. Her identity was a fake. Frederique Bonlieu, aged 33, geomorphologist, was in fact Lieutenant Christine Cabon, an army officer seconded to the DGSE, France's secret service. She had been invalided out of Le Cadre Spécial, an elite commando unit, after a parachute jumping accident three years earlier and had been transferred to the DGSE and trained as an infiltrator.

Her mission of infiltrating the Auckland office of Greenpeace was tame compared to her previous assignments. One had been to penetrate the Palestine Liberation Organisation in Lebanon. She worked as an interpreter and lived with PLO members and when her mission was completed in 1984, she underwent plastic surgery for her own safety.

What could she find out from Greenpeace? It was an organisation without secrets; it had an open-door policy towards anyone who was interested in ecology.

'It must have been rather boring — we have nothing to hide,' Shaw recalled later. 'Greenpeace is just a vehicle to vent their frustration and anger at . . . anger at the whole Pacific for being anti-nuclear and anti-French colonialism. It is just sour grapes.'

The small Greenpeace office was rather hectic and few people had a chance to take much notice of the talkative Frenchwoman. The *Rainbow Warrior* was due to arrive in less than three months and there was much planning still to be done. Dutch campaigner Rein Achterberg was organising a protest flotilla of four peace yachts which would travel with the *Warrior* to Moruroa. Others were working on plans for the Pacific voyage, or busy lobbying against the manufacture and use of the toxic spray 245-T. In one room, somebody was writing a newsletter about the Antarctic campaign planned for later in the year — another campaign aimed at France which two years before had destroyed a penguin colony to build an airstrip in Adèlie Land.

Later, Shaw went with Cabon for a meal at a nearby café, expecting they would share the bill.

'I don't have any money,' Cabon said, after they had eaten. It became common for Greenpeace members to pay for her. Was it because of a tight-fisted DGSE budget, or just part of the cover?

Shaw arranged for Cabon to stay the following night at the home of Greenpeace national coordinator Carol Stewart, in the inner city suburb of Grey Lynn.

Stewart found it puzzling that a woman who professed to be an environmentalist should have such conservative views on nuclear power and independence in the Pacific. While many Greenpeace members, including Stewart, supported the Kanaks in the elections to be held in New Caledonia during September, Cabon said she hoped they would lose heavily. (In fact, in the ballot on 29 September the Kanak Socialist National Liberation Front [FLNKS] won power in three out of the four new regional governments, a milestone in their campaign to become independent in 1987.)

'Here you are very far from your enemies. In Europe, we are very close,' Cabon told Auckland journalist Jenny Little. 'Trying to find peace with weapons is a very big paradox but without this defence, we risk becoming like Finland, which is so influenced by Russia,' she said. 'Since we've had nuclear weapons we haven't been threatened nationally.'

Many Greenpeace activists were surprised at her views and they asked her what brought her to the Pacific where anti-nuclear feeling was so strong. Cabon told them that while her main purpose in visiting New Zealand was a professional interest in geography and archaeology, she wanted to learn more about the Pacific. She said she was going to a conference about coral reefs in Tahiti in late May and she also wanted tourist information for a group of colleagues who would visit the country later.

Cabon frequently wanted to remain alone in the Grey Lynn house while Stewart and her other flatmates went out. She would have had plenty of time to rifle through Stewart's room looking for files and other pieces of information she might have taken home from the office. (However, Stewart never kept files at home; Cabon would have found only telex messages at the Grey Lynn house.)

She cleverly avoided being photographed and she revealed little about her personal life. Although she liked women, she was cool towards men. Stewart thought it odd that a woman of her age had no address in Paris, her home. All the Greenpeace campaigners discovered about her past life was that she had worked in Senegal as an 'archaeologist'.

She insisted on speaking French whenever possible — her grasp of English was rather poor. It seemed like a good idea therefore to introduce her to other supporters who knew French. After staying with Stewart for almost two weeks, Cabon moved into a Kingsland house with Greenpeace campaigner Jane Cooper and *New Zealand Herald* reporter Karen Mangnall. Both Cooper and Mangnall had extensive experience of the South Pacific and its independence movements.

Cabon busied herself in the Greenpeace office, doing translations into French of some of the ecology group's campaign literature and preparing articles on the Pacific for French newspapers — articles which nobody ever saw, written or published.

She also listened. When Stewart, Shaw, Achterberg, Judy Seaboyer and other officials discussed strategy for the Moruroa campaign she tried to be within hearing. When telex messages came in from the *Rainbow Warrior* in the Marshall Islands about plans and contacts with the Vanuatu Government, Cabon was able to keep the DGSE posted with developments.

But some of the work she did for Greenpeace was in conflict with the views she expressed. With a Dutch activist, Monique Davis, she translated the script from a controversial half-hour film documentary called *Behind the Flower Curtain*,[1] produced by Tahitian nationalist Henri Hiro. It was about the cultural, social and economic imperialism of France in Polynesia.

She also insisted on rephrasing an 'open letter' to President Mitterrand from French citizens living in New Zealand. She said Greenpeace was too hard line and she would word the letter in a way that would be more palatable to the presidential Elysée Palace. The letter said:

Are we your enemies? Could you not find a solution which gives us back our French pride? A solution directed towards disarmament which, by its greatness and generosity, would set an example of a peaceful country among the most military powers, whose natural position is to defend freedom and human rights. A position which, unfortunately, France has not taken while we have been living here.

The letter was circulated among French nationals, but gained only two signatures and was never sent to Mitterrand.

Meanwhile, Cabon was gathering information about the coastline. Equipped with a 35 mm camera, she began taking photographs of Auckland's wharves and bought several maps of the city and its harbour. On several 'sightseeing' trips she travelled around Northland, Coromandel and the East Coast, looking for a suitable landing spot for DGSE agents. The information was regularly sent to Paris, sometimes by telephone.

One day Cabon had an unusual request for Carol Stewart. 'Carol, could you phone around some diving shops to find out the cost of diving equipment for me?' she asked. 'I've got some friends coming on a tourism trip later in the year and I'll need the information for them.'

'Okay,' Stewart replied. 'But why do you need me to phone?'

Cabon said she had difficulty understanding details on the phone. She asked Stewart to find out the cost of hiring oxygen diving tanks and filling them. Cabon also wanted to know where small boats and dinghies could be hired. Patiently, Stewart pieced together the information for her.

Later Cabon sent these details, together with information she had gathered about campervan, yacht and car hire, and maps and photographs, to a post office box number in Paris. A secret DGSE number.

'Why did she do it from the Greenpeace office?' Elaine Shaw asked later. 'Was it her twisted sense of humour? Or was it a bizarre way of getting back at us?'

Certainly, Cabon was sure of not being unmasked. The Greenpeace office volunteers were too busy to pay special attention to her.

The night before Cabon flew to Tahiti on 24 May, she hosted Shaw, Stewart and some of the other activists for a farewell drink in De Bretts wine bar, a couple of blocks from the Greenpeace office. In spite of a boycott of French products, Cabon bought a bottle of beaujolais to share with her 'friends'.

In Papeete, Cabon registered at the Reef and Mankind Congress but went only for the last day and was clearly out of her depth as a so-called geologist. At the conference she met Swedish anthropologist Dr Bengt Danielsson and his French wife Marie-Thérèse, both outspoken anti-nuclear campaigners. Dr Danielsson, a crew member on the *Kon Tiki* raft voyage in 1947 from South America to Polynesia, had settled in Tahiti and was also a supporter of Greenpeace.

Before leaving Auckland, Cabon had noted letters from Danielsson written earlier in the year. He had discussed Greenpeace New Zealand's plans for the *Rainbow Warrior's* protest voyage to Moruroa.

Elaine Shaw had had vague talks with Tahitian anti-nuclear campaigners of possibilities which included visiting

Huahine Island and picking up islander activists, taking doctors to the atolls near Moruroa, and linking up with a small flotilla of Tahitian protest boats and canoes. Cabon apparently interpreted this as an 'invasion'.

When the *Warrior* was bombed, Cabon was in Israel on an archaeological dig at Pardes Hanna. She sent a letter to Elaine Shaw a week after the blasts which said:

> The news about the sunk [sic] of the *Rainbow Warrior* just reached me. . . . What can I say after such news? I feel so chocked [sic]! If the French Government is behind this work, he has probably missed his goal because I see two French newspapers and never the popularity of Greenpeace has been so important or so well defended . . . Why such a monstrosity!?
>   Could you say to everybody in Auckland that I am with you, with all my heart.
>   Love
>   Frederique

By the time the letter arrived in New Zealand, the police had exposed Cabon. The *Auckland Star* revealed the news on 26 July without actually naming her: 'French Spy May Have Infiltrated Greenpeace'.

Cabon turned out to be a key figure in the sabotage plot.

Christine Cabon's reports to Paris became nails in the *Rainbow Warrior's* coffin. Senior officers at DGSE headquarters were having little difficulty getting approval for their plan to sink the peace ship. The French position in the South Pacific was going from bad to worse: the Kanaks were well on the way to achieving their goal of an independent Kanaky republic and Tahitian activists were following the Kanaks' lead. Greenpeace had already created problems at Moruroa on its four previous protest voyages but this time it was protesting on a far bigger scale. The *Rainbow Warrior* was no vulnerable little yacht; it was big enough to seriously embarrass the French Navy and there would also be a flotilla of boats accompanying her. It would be difficult and costly to police them during the neutron bomb tests planned for later in the year.

French Defence Minister Charles Hernu had heard late in 1984 of Greenpeace's protest plans. He 'exploded with fury', and ordered a detailed dossier from his security services about the *Warrior*. Admiral Henri Fages, director of the Centre d'Expérimentation du Pacifique,[2] and the DGSE chief, Admiral Pierre Lacoste, reported to Hernu in January 1985 that Greenpeace planned to sail an 'armada' of small boats into French territorial waters around Moruroa. Their report speculated that the *Warrior* might be equipped with the latest devices for evaluating French progress on the neutron bomb — and perhaps could even sabotage the tests. Another extraordinary speculation was that Greenpeace was being secretly financed by British Petroleum in the hope that it would hinder French development of nuclear power and preserve Britain's European market for North Sea oil.

Cabon's reports heightened the French military's fears — even though she had access to information which should have allayed them, including an order by Greenpeace International chairman David McTaggart that the *Warrior* should not breach the 12-mile territorial limit around Moruroa.

'If she is taken inside, the shit is going to hit the fan,' McTaggart said. But the DGSE had already made up its mind to stop the *Warrior* at any cost.

Top-level meetings, including some at the Elysée, were attended by General Jean Saulnier, head of the presidential military secretariat, and General Jeannou Lacaze, chief of staff of the French Army. A contingency plan was drawn up to *anticiper* ('to neutralise') the Greenpeace mission. One report presented to Hernu recommended the sinking of the *Warrior* with mines and budgeted for a team of frogmen, supported by a submarine, to carry out the operation for less than $1 million.

Two army colonels were dispatched to New Zealand in March to assess its feasibility and Christine Cabon was sent the following month to make detailed reports.

The French secret service grew out of the resistance movement of the Second World War. Their headquarters is dubbed *La Piscine* because the former army barracks on Boulevard Mortier, on the north-east fringe of Paris, is close to the neighbourhood swimming pool. The DGSE has largely restricted its international activities to French-speaking Africa, Eastern Europe, the Middle East and the South Pacific.

Tiny compared to Britain's MI6, the United States' CIA or the Soviets' KGB, the DGSE has been plagued by scandal and has frequently been at the centre of both daring and bungled operations. In one of its more spectacular successes, the Service de Documentation Extérieure et de Contre-Espionage, which spawned the DGSE, sank the freighter *Atlas*, loaded with arms for pro-independence guerrillas in Algeria, in Hamburg harbour during September 1958. In a similar operation, the *Alkaira* and its cargo were sunk off Ostend during April the following year.

The most serious blot on the record of the French secret service was the Ben Barka affair. Moroccan Opposition leader Mehdi Ben Barka, a highly respected Third World spokesman, was betrayed by France after it had given him asylum. Although the SDECE tried to blame Ben Barka's kidnapping and subsequent murder in 1965 on the judicial police, evidence pointed to the secret service as being the real culprit.

Another notorious incident was in July 1983 when nearly 100 mercenaries were sent to Chad to aid the embattled government of France's ally, Hissene Habre, against rebel forces backed by Libyan troops. The mercenaries — recruited by a former DGSE colonel, René Dulac — looted the countryside and terrorised local people. They had to be withdrawn shortly after landing.

Under the jurisdiction of the Defence Ministry, the DGSE (as the secret service was renamed in 1982) has 2,000 officers and agents. It is a far cry from just before the Second World War, when France had only 50 agents. Then the spies received orders from the army's Deuxième Bureau which concentrated its attention on Germany and Britain, the latter a rival to France in the Middle East. It was during the Nazi occupation that the modern secret service was created by General Charles de Gaulle's Free French forces.

By the end of the war, the service had swelled to 10,000 agents, but had become inefficient and corrupt. Immediately the Germans were driven out of Paris by the Allied forces, the service seized all property which had been in the hands of the occupiers, including 123 apartment buildings and more than 1,400 vehicles. More than 8,000 agents were purged in December 1945 when the SDECE was created.

Reorganised as the DGSE in 1982 when the socialists came to power, the service's official statute requires it to 'obtain and exploit information and documents concerning the security of France and to detect and obstruct activities working in France's disfavour'. The DGSE is only a quarter of the size of its British equivalent. It has an annual budget of less than $70 million and has only recently adopted a computer-based information system. During the reorganisation in 1982, chief Pierre Marion was sacked and replaced by Admiral Lacoste.

The DGSE is split into three branches. Firstly, there is an intelligence division which processes information from agents in the field or gleaned from radio and telephone surveillance. This branch is known to be active in the South Pacific. The second division is responsible for counter-espionage with the task of recruiting agents among France's adversaries, or inciting defections from their services.

Most important and most notorious of the three branches is the Action Service. Dependent on the other branches for information, it is otherwise autonomous, except for the approval of its operations budget by the central office. It is a complex organisation whose activities are carried out by civil and military staff, 'honorary correspondents' — such as diplomats, military advisers or French businessmen abroad — or by hired 'casuals'. The latter are regularly trained by the DGSE but are not officially listed on the staff and can therefore be disowned if an operation backfires.

While the *Rainbow Warrior* was evacuating the Rongelap Islanders, the operation to sink her was already under way. An emergency fund available from the office of the Prime Minister, Laurent Fabius, had been used on the authority of Hernu and Saulnier. The Action Service was now on the job.

Navy reservist Dr Xavier Maniguet, 38, a skilled underwater swimmer and a specialist in diving medicine, approached the Odyssée Travel Agency in Paris to request a charter boat from New Caledonia to New Zealand. He also needed some companions.

A few days later, a Raymond Velche, describing himself as a professional skipper, told the travel agency he and two friends were also looking for a Noumea charter yacht and needed a fourth crewman. Velche's real identity was Chief Petty Officer Roland Verge, a 32-year-old DGSE training officer at the crack army frogman school in Aspretto, Corsica. His companions were Petty Officer Gerald Andries (alias photographer Eric Audrenc), 32, and Petty Officer Jean-Michel Barcelo (alias salesman Jean-Michel Berthelo), 33.

Through Odyssée, they found the yacht they needed — the $100,000 *Ouvéa*, a 12-metre French-built First 38, which had been stolen a couple of years previously and recovered in Darwin. Verge flew out to Noumea to check out the yacht while Andries went to London. Andries' job was to purchase an inflatable dinghy and an engine. He paid $3,000 cash for a grey and black French-made Zodiac and a four horsepower Yamaha engine in the name of a bogus Belgian diving company at the north London firm of Barnet Marine. Verge confirmed the $18,000 charter of the *Ouvéa* with the owners, Noumea Yacht Charters.

Verge, Andries and Barcelo were given a final briefing by their Aspretto base commander, 48-year-old Lieutenant-Colonel Louis-Pierre Dillais. He would join the three in both New Caledonia and New Zealand to oversee the sabotage operation. Also briefed were a woman and a man who would travel on false Swiss passports as a honey-mooning couple, Sophie and Alain Turenge. In reality they were Captain Dominique Prieur, 36, Christine Cabon's superior and a specialist in European pacifist and 'green' movements, and Major Alain Mafart, 34, deputy commander at Aspretto.

On 7 June, Verge, Andries and Barcelo flew to Noumea and prepared for their voyage south. Dillais, alias Phillippe Dubast, an analyst from Rheims, arrived on the same flight. Four days later Dr Maniguet joined his crewmates. After picking up magnetic mines and other equipment, they left for New Zealand on 13 June — the day the *Rainbow Warrior* left Majuro Atoll for Kiribati.

The *Ouvéa* arrived on 22 June at the deserted harbour of Parengarenga in the Far North during a storm. It was unusual for any foreign yacht to visit the treacherous, exposed harbour and the crew hadn't reckoned on their arrival being reported by one of the few local residents to park ranger Hector Crene. The ranger phoned Opua customs and then briefly visited the *Ouvéa*.

The same day the 'Turenges' flew into Auckland from London and later hired a Toyota campervan for picking up the sabotage gear. On 23 June Colonel Dillais arrived from Noumea, now alias Jean-Louis Dormand.

Covering the 160-kilometre stretch of sea before reaching customs in Opua, the *Ouvéa* had a choice of many 'smugglers' coves' for hiding the sabotage equipment ashore. Five days after Dillais arrived, the *Ouvéa* moored at Whangarei — and the crew lived it up with dining, wine and women.

Dillais drove around Northland for a few days and returned to Auckland on 4 July. He booked into a seventh-floor room in the Hyatt Kingsgate Hotel with a view of Marsden Wharf where the *Rainbow Warrior*, now on her way from Vanuatu, would dock. Three days later he was able to watch the Peace Squadron and other yachts welcome the *Warrior* to Auckland.

The *Ouvéa* left Whangarei on the morning of 9 July and the crew radioed that they expected to reach Norfolk

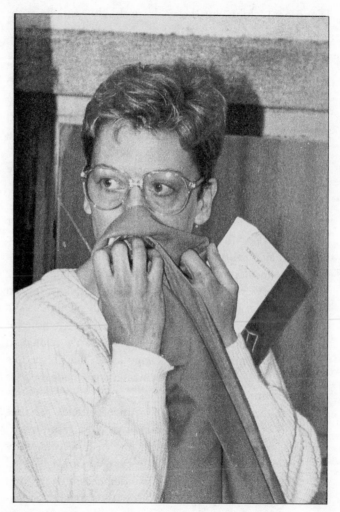

Above: *Major Alain Mafart (alias Alain Turenge). A DGSE agent, formerly deputy commander of the secret underwater frogman school in Aspretto, Corsica. He arrived in New Zealand on a false Swiss passport.* (Auckland Star)

Right: *Captain Dominique Prieur (alias Sophie Turenge). A controller in the DGSE's intelligence gathering and evaluation wing, she specialised in European 'green' and pacifist movements.* (Auckland Star)

Island on 14 July. But the yacht probably headed south, anchoring off Leigh, and left for Norfolk Island shortly before the bombing.

When Hobson Bay yachtsmen vigilantes phoned the police about a strange Zodiac dinghy on the night of 10 July, it took the police almost 20 minutes to arrive and by then the campervan had gone. But the yachtsmen had noted the number plate and their description of the man in the dinghy later identified him as Barcelo.

Barely two-and-a-half hours later, the *Warrior* lay crippled on the seabed, sabotaged by a double bomb blast.

Prime Minister David Lange branded the bombing a major criminal act with political or terrorist overtones. He promised every effort would be made to catch the attackers. He also considered sending a Royal New Zealand Navy frigate to Moruroa but then rejected the idea as an 'extraordinary militarisation' of a peaceful protest.

'Greenpeace, of course, have enemies for a whole lot of causes around the world — not necessarily related to France or the nuclear issue,' Lange said. 'They're people whose causes are varied and they would have made millions of friends and dozens of enemies.'

Vanuatu, which had a government official, Charles Rara, on board the bombed ship, was even more blunt. Prime Minister Walter Lini, who had in June personally welcomed the *Rainbow Warrior* to Port Vila and endorsed the protest voyage to Moruroa, condemned the bombing. He blamed 'stupid people who don't understand Green-

peace's work towards peace'. Some Vanuatu Government officials said the bombing could have been masterminded by wealthy French business interests bitterly opposed to Kanak independence.

Greenpeace made a vow to continue the fight for a nuclear-free Pacific. The five world directors of the organisation held a telephone conference and resolved to carry on the campaign with the *Vega* leading the fleet.

'If they wanted to intimidate us by killing one of our people it will only increase our resolve,' Dr Patrick Moore, one of the directors, said. 'They've got no satisfaction from their act of terrorism.' (He wasn't quite sure who *they* were at that stage.)

Later, it was decided to divert the 58-metre ocean-going tug *Greenpeace* to Moruroa. The tug was being prepared to go to the Antarctic to set up the world's first non-governmental base camp there.

The *Auckland Star* denounced the Pacific 'escalation of hate' which had spread to New Zealand. It said:

With an irrationality that is impossible to fathom, [mad bombers] have struck at crusaders whose tactics have always been non-violent, whose aims have always been to preserve and enhance life on our planet in campaigns ranging from saving endangered whales to opposing nuclear weapons testing.

The Greenpeace organisation has always found a soft spot in our national heart, pursuing, as it has, the campaign against French testing in the Pacific, which we as a nation led a decade ago with the dispatch of a frigate to the testing grounds.

But even as terrorist acts go, this must count as one of the most pointless. To blow up a boat dedicated to putting the peace back into the Pacific is not going to win any friends for the perpetrators. Just the opposite.

Shocked New Zealanders poured donations into trust funds set up to replace the *Rainbow Warrior* and for Fernando Pereira's two children, and raised $200,000 in five months.

But it wasn't all sympathy. 'Good luck *Rainbow Warrior* . . . Pacific will not be Lebanon,' said a letter sent to the Greenpeace office. 'Pacifists, hooligans, hippies, trade unions, PLO, Khomeinists, Labour, terrorists — all the same riff-raff, all KGB agents.' The slogan around the death's head motif at the top of the letter read: 'Revenge. Better dead than red. No more Vietnams'.

New Zealand police began their biggest manhunt which involved more than 100 detectives and stretched across the South Pacific from Papeete to Sydney and Norfolk Island to Noumea. But Detective Superintendent Allan Galbraith, the quietly spoken Scottish-born chief of the investigation was cautious, even though it was already suspected that limpet mines had been used to sink the ship.

'If it is proved to be bombs — and we're working on that assumption — it would certainly be unusual for New Zealand. It must be the first bombing of this kind,' he said. The 48-year-old police officer had been in New Zealand's crack armed offenders squad for 10 years and had later studied terrorist sabotage techniques with Scotland Yard's bomb squad.

The *Warrior* was the third ship to be blown up in a New Zealand harbour. The Castle-class trawler *Hautapu* was bombed before dawn on 2 June 1966 and the attackers were never traced. In November 1983 a 10-metre fishing boat sank at an Opotiki wharf mooring. The boat's hull had been ripped open by a time bomb during a drug feud.

Early leads in Operation Rainbow indicated a French connection. As forensic experts examined the black-and-grey Zodiac found in Hobson Bay, navy divers searched for more clues. They discovered the abandoned Yamaha engine and later the first of two small oxygen bottles with French markings. The bottle, used with rebreather gear to prevent surface bubbles, showed it was a professional sabotage operation. Police also traced the number plate of the campervan sighted in Hobson Bay to one hired by the Turenges.

On 12 July, two days after the bombing, came the first official French reaction. Political counsellor Charles Montan of the French Embassy in Wellington said: 'In no way is France involved. The French Government doesn't deal with its opponents in such ways.'

Meanwhile the Turenges arrived at the Newman's hire agency in the Auckland suburb of Mt Wellington to return their van. They asked for a refund because they were returning the van early. Office worker Becky Hayter phoned the police and kept them occupied until the police arrived.

The pair were questioned and three days later were charged with having false passports. They insisted on their being Swiss, although Swiss authorities denied this.

While police systematically checked the movements of all French people in the country, they took a special interest in Francois Verlet who was on board the *Warrior* about the time they believed the bombs had been planted on the ship's hull. Police in Tahiti were asked to detain him for questioning. But he later told a New Zealand policeman he was a militant pacifist who supported Greenpeace. He eventually disappeared.

By now the police had their eyes on the *Ouvéa* which had arrived at Norfolk Island. Nine detectives were sent there on 16 July to interview the crew. But they arrived two hours after Dr Maniguet had flown to Sydney. (He later returned to France through Singapore, denying any involvement.) Three detectives were also sent to Noumea.

The detectives on Norfolk took scrapings from the yacht's bilges to check for explosives. They also found a map of Auckland with a Ponsonby address handwritten on it — later shown to be a map sent by Christine Cabon to the DGSE. But Verge, Andries and Barcelo claimed they were tourists and even though they were convinced the crew had false passports, the detectives were forced to let them go under pressure from the local police for lack of evidence.

Claiming to be headed for Noumea, the *Ouvéa* crew set sail later that day. The last radio contact apparently made with the yacht was 6.20 a.m. on 21 July when it was reported to be 50 kilometres north-west of the tourist resort Île des Pins in New Caledonia. In fact, by then they had probably been picked up at sea and the yacht scuttled.

A nuclear-powered hunter-killer submarine, *Rubis*, had docked in Noumea on 10 May — the first visit to the South Pacific by a French nuclear warship. It left Noumea on 5 July, and although its top speed of 25 knots was fast enough to get it from Noumea to Tahiti in less than a week, it arrived in Fare Ute port on 22 July, almost three weeks later.

Tahitian sources claimed Verge, Andries and Barcelo were taken on board the *Rubis* and then transported to France by military aircraft, but the French Navy denied being involved. According to the navy publication *Cols Bleus* (Blue Collars), the *Rubis* spent several days in the Coral Sea and could have easily made a rendezvous with the *Ouvéa*.

On 24 July police charged Sophie and Alain Turenge with murder, arson and conspiracy to commit arson, in addition to the passport charges. The murder charge covered the death of Fernando Pereira and the arson charges the use of explosives. Two days later the police issued arrest warrants with the same charges against Verge, Andries and Barcelo — but under their false identities.

From the map found on the *Ouvéa*, the police deduced that Frederique Bonlieu had been a mole for the DGSE in

Right: *While police investigations proceed, salvage operations get underway. Here, Davey Edward looks on as the 600 hp Detroit engine is lifted up through the smokestack. Edward believed it was possible to refit the ship and make her seaworthy again.* (Gil Hanly)

Greenpeace. After newspaper reports of these suspicions, the DGSE sent a coded telegram on 27 July to Tel Aviv where Christine Cabon was taking part in an archaeological dig. It said: 'Your Father Is Sick, Come Home'.

Cabon, whose father had died several years before, immediately took a TWA flight from Tel Aviv to Paris. On the same day, a telegram arrived at the Israeli police ministry from Auckland police asking that Cabon be detained in custody so a New Zealand police officer could question her. Later, Superintendent Galbraith claimed she had still been in Israel when the telegram arrived, which raised questions of Israeli complicity in her escape.

Accusations were now being made in France against the French Government. Within hours of the weekly magazines *Vendredi, Samedi, Dimanche* and *L'Evénement du Jeudi* accusing the DGSE of having planned the sabotage operation and unmasking Sophie Turenge as a spy, President Mitterrand on 8 August ordered Prime Minister Fabius to conduct a 'rigorous inquiry'.

The magazines also said the *DGSE* had decided to disable the *Warrior* when it had learned she was equipped with scientific instruments able to record and analyse scheduled neutron bomb tests at Moruroa.

Left: *Greenpeace campaigners on the steps of the Auckland District Court after the 'Turenges' were charged with murder, sabotage and conspiracy on 24 July. From left: Rainbow Warrior skipper Peter Willcox, international director Steve Sawyer, Fleur Hopkins and Kelly Rigg.* (Auckland Star)

'To any seismologist this would be patently absurd,' Steve Sawyer said. The only piece of equipment on board for monitoring radiation was a simple 'nuke buster', a $200 radiation detector Sawyer had bought to take on the voyage to Rongelap Atoll.

The French Government named 65-year-old Bernard Tricot, who was secretary-general of the Elysée Palace during General De Gaulle's final years in power, to carry out the investigation and Mitterrand wrote a letter to David Lange, saying:

Information . . . indicates that a link could exist between French agencies and two people charged by judicial authorities in New Zealand in the affair of the *Rainbow Warrior*. One can only wait . . . to find out how accurate this information is and what person might be held responsible. Nonetheless, I wish to tell you . . . how much I and the Government of the republic abhor the criminal attack committed on your territory which no excuse can justify . . .

The Prime Minister, M. Laurent Fabius, has given orders for all possible extra help to be given your investigations, while we are also naturally pursuing our own. I intend that this matter should be handled with the greatest possible severity and that your country should be able to count on the full collaboration of France.

Then the dissemination of false information began. It is a practice of the French secret service to recruit journalists as 'honourable correspondents', or part-time undercover agents. According to Pascal Krop, a journalist with *L'Evénement du Jeudi* and co-author of a history[3] of the French intelligence services, there are as many as 50 journalists who are DGSE collaborators.

After *VSD* and *L'Evénement* accused the Turenges of being DGSE agents, a journalist with the Government-owned radio network France Inter, Gilbert Picard, said on air that he had read the orders handed to the Turenges and their assignment was simply one of 'observation' on behalf of the Government agency charged with security for the nuclear test sites. He blamed the bombing on MI6. The story was repeated by other French and international media.

Le Matin, the newspaper bought by friends of President Mitterrand and now edited by his former press secretary Max Gallo, printed allegations of MI6 involvement in the bombing and that the Soviet KGB had infiltrated Greenpeace. This claim was repeated by the Australian and New Zealand news media. Bryan Boswell, of the national newspaper the *Australian*, wrote:

It is remotely conceivable that if the KGB did have someone on board the *Rainbow Warrior* he or she might be privy to information useful to the Soviet Union. . . . Some equipment capable of being used for espionage could have been placed on board.

And as for a spy — if Greenpeace had not realised that Bonlieu was a spy for the French why should they be aware of a spy for the Russians as part of their crew? As a theory it is at least as credible to many Frenchmen as that of a secret service running rampant and deliberately laying clues to point the finger of blame at its own Government.

In another report, *Le Matin* blamed the bombing on DONS, the South African secret service, with possible MI6 or CIA help.

One of the worst inventions was a six-page story carried by *Paris-Match* magazine claiming to prove Greenpeace was planning an 'invasion' of Moruroa Atoll and therefore France was justified in defending itself against the *Rainbow Warrior*. The magazine had a double-page spread showing a photograph of a red-painted landing craft on the deck of the tug *Greenpeace*, which was being prepared for the Antarctic expedition. Ignoring the fact that the landing craft was a type commonly used by scientific teams, *Paris-Match* noted the tug was replacing the *Warrior* for the Moruroa protest and said:

THE GAME'S UP
This photograph accuses: on the boat deck of the *Greenpeace*, on its way to Moruroa, is a landing craft. Instead of the traditional Zodiacs used by the anti-whaling campaigners, the 'pacifist' navy is now carrying military equipment . . . The presence of the landing craft confirms the information that the Pacific Experiments Centre had sent to Paris last January that Greenpeace planned to invade Moruroa, with ecologists and Polynesians trying to recapture the atoll.

Over an article by right-wing businessman Paul-Loup Sulitzer, the magazine carried the headline: 'Moscow Triumphs: The French Secret Services Have Been Torn Apart!'

More than a scandal, it's a tragedy which is being played out in front of us. It is putting at stake: our policy of nuclear deterrence; the key to the security of our country; the credibility of the men in the highest positions of the state; the image of our army as a whole. In other words, our only means to freedom!

In the same vein, local French television in Tahiti screened part of a documentary about the Rongelap evacuation made by journalists Walter Guerin and Philippe Chatenay. But the commentary said: 'Polynesians from the atolls around Moruroa embarking on the *Rainbow Warrior* to take part in an invasion of the nuclear base'. *Le Point* news magazine ran a story saying: 'The Swedish ecologist and longtime resident of Tahiti, Bengt Danielsson, had organised an invasion of Moruroa, to be carried out by the inhabitants of neighbouring atolls with the help of *pirogues* [canoes] and dinghies.' It said the DGSE had been opening his mail.

Dr Danielsson angrily denied the story in an open letter to a Tahitian newspaper, but the magazine did not publish an apology.

One variation of the story of MI6 involvement was that the real culprits were British *agents provocateurs* who had deliberately strewn the beaches around Auckland with incriminating gear marked 'Made in France'. Their motive, according to this version of events, was to get even with the French for their sale of Exocet rockets to Argentina during the Falklands war.

Politicians also added to the rumours. During a debate on New Caledonia in the Senate chamber in Paris, a conservative politician, Charles Pasqua, Senate whip of the Rassemblement pour la République (RPR) party, accused New Zealand of supplying arms and other equipment to saboteurs infiltrating the territory.

'Who is likely to believe the military act without orders? France is not a banana republic,' Pasqua said. 'If the secret service is not involved, then why do we accept the arrogance and impudence of New Zealand and its interference in our territory?' He demanded that Fabius resign if it were proved the French secret service was involved.

It was the first time Fabius was challenged. But it seemed that Defence Minister Charles Hernu's career was at risk.

Bernard Tricot's report was made public on 26 August. He confirmed the identities of six agents operating in New Zealand — including the *Ouvéa* crew who were now in Paris. He said they had been authorised to infiltrate Greenpeace and to consider ways to counter the ecology group's activities, but not to carry out any action. 'At the present state of information,' he said, he believed Dominique Prieur and Alain Mafart to be innocent. But he later added that he just might have been deceived!

David Lange demanded an immediate apology for the 'outrageous violation of our sovereignty' by the spies. He suggested that French Ambassador Jacques Bourgoin might be recalled to Paris and added that the report could hardly be called a whitewash, it was so transparent.

'About the only useful statement made by Mr Tricot . . . is that a more thorough investigation is required,' complained the *New Zealand Herald*. It said that seldom could any government or security agency have been made to look as 'squeaky clean' as did the French. 'Even if Mr Tricot were to pour all the perfume of Provence on the episode it would still come out stinking like a skunk.'

The *Auckland Star* said French authorities must believe New Zealanders were 'gullible if they expect us to swallow what can only be described as a half-baked report' on the bombing. 'This can only further harm New Zealand-French relations and the image of the French in the Pacific. It can hardly be regarded as the act of a *friendly* nation.'

Opposition leader Jim McLay cancelled a planned visit to France. Two New Zealand policemen were posted as guards for the New Zealand consul-general, Sarah Dennis, in Noumea following threats by extremist white New Caledonian settlers.

The French 'greens' issued a statement which said: 'M. Tricot, the secretary-general of the Elysée from 1959 to 1969, a period during which the cloak-and-dagger boys and the parallel police had a free hand in France, remains a faithful servant of the state, competent and silent. He has done his job well!'

Hostility towards France grew, especially following a threat by President Mitterrand that the protest flotilla from New Zealand would face arrest when it reached Moruroa. The warning coincided with President Mitterrand's refusal to meet David McTaggart. The leftwing French newspaper

Libération declared: 'The shadow of Watergate now hovers over sweet France,' referring to the scandal which drove Richard Nixon from the United States presidency.

Le Point claimed that 10 mercenaries recruited in London and Paris had been duped into joining the *Rainbow Warrior* operation as a diversion. One of the mercenaries told the magazine he had been recruited on behalf of wealthy European settlers in New Caledonia to 'defend' them from Kanaks seeking independence. He said he was suspicious about the mission. He and another man, codenamed Chabnes, were two French mercenaries who arrived in New Zealand in early July to prepare for the bombing. They were hired by a Paris agency run by Colonel Dulac, the man behind the 1983 Chad fiasco. Both were described in the magazine as experts in 'operation preparation' and they later went into hiding in France.

On 5 September, Fabius ordered a fresh investigation into the bombing, saying he wanted the 'truth'. Two weeks later, in a defiant rebuff to the South Pacific Forum nations which in August had adopted the nuclear-free Treaty of Rarotonga, President Mitterrand flew to Moruroa Atoll to meet French ambassadors, high commissioners and other senior officials in a South Pacific summit. Both Australian Prime Minister Bob Hawke and Lange saw the trip as provocative and arrogant.

Lange said Mitterrand had declared New Zealand an

Left: *The DSGE disclosures became the butt of satiric barbs by cartoonists.* (Malcolm Walker/New Outlook)

'enemy' when a presidential spokesman said opponents of France's nuclear tests would be ignored and anybody opposing French interests would be seen as adversaries. 'It should properly be translated as *enemies*,' Lange said.

An invitation by Mitterrand for South Pacific leaders to visit Moruroa also drew a frosty response. Hawke, Lange, Fiji's Ratu Sir Kamisese Mara and Western Samoa's Tofilau Eti were among leaders who rejected the offer. 'I want to see Mitterrand — not look down a bomb crater,' said Lange, who offered to meet the French president in an attempt to defuse the row.

Less than a week later, on 19 September, the 62-year-old Hernu, one of Mitterrand's closest associates for 25 years, resigned and Admiral Pierre Lacoste was sacked. The *Herald* greeted the news with the banner headline: 'Adieu Monsieur Hernu!'

Four days later, Fabius admitted DGSE agents had sunk the *Rainbow Warrior* and that they were acting under orders. His admission followed claims by the London *Sunday Times* that Mitterrand and Fabius had known in advance of the bombing, and by *Le Monde* that a third spy team had been operating in New Zealand. The latter report probably meant operation chief Colonel Dillais and possibly others.

David Lange described the bombing as a 'sordid act of international state-backed terrorism' and said the French Government would face an unprecedented claim for an 'affront to sovereignty'. France was expected to face a bill totalling more than $20 million, covering the replacement cost of the *Rainbow Warrior* and up to $3 million for the investigation, during which police had worked for more than 70,000 hours and travelled almost 200,000 kilometres.

Even the French press wasn't much kinder. Not renowned for aggressive reporting, it had nevertheless ferreted out many embarrassing facts in the face of a stubborn Government silence. Inevitably, comparisons were made with Watergate. Headlines such as 'Underwatergate' . . . 'Watergaffe' . . . and 'Watergate-Sur-Seine' were used by American and European newspapers.

The French Government's about-face came after the new Defence Minister Paul Quilès discovered parts of the relevant DGSE files were missing and ordered them replaced. Quilès, 43, is a gifted leftwing administrator who has been compared with the ruthless eighteenth-century revolutionary Robespierre (his nickname is 'Robespaul'), and it took him less than 48 hours to discover what had been hidden from Fabius and Mitterrand for 10 weeks.

General René Imbot, the stocky new chief of the DGSE, said he had unearthed a plot to destroy his agency but after five soldiers, including a DGSE colonel, had been charged with leaking defence secrets he claimed the secret service had been 'locked up'.

Greenpeace was not satisfied with France's admission of responsibility for the bombing. David McTaggart called on Mitterrand to turn his attention from blame and concentrate on the 'real issue' — France's nuclear testing in the South Pacific.

For the crew of the *Rainbow Warrior*, the sinking of the ship, Pereira's death and the political intrigue was a startling contrast to the humanitarian mission they had been involved in. Skipper Peter Willcox and crew member Grace O'Sullivan joined the *Vega* on its protest voyage to Moruroa; radio operator Lloyd Anderson was on board the cutter *Varangian*; Bunny McDiarmid flew to Curaçao to join the *Greenpeace*. Others coped with the difficult task of cleaning out equipment for scrap and preparing the ship for burial at sea.

'It's important to connect the bombing in Auckland with what is happening in the Pacific,' engineer Hanne Sorensen said. 'We will take the struggle for a nuclear-free Pacific to those who oppose it — the handful of people in nuclear capitals like Washington and Paris who have no right to destroy our planet.'

As the protest flotilla boats left one by one for Moruroa, New Zealand columnist W.P. Reeves wrote in the *Dominion*:

The principal weakness of the idea to destroy the *Rainbow Warrior*, however cocked-up the execution, though was that the sinking was never likely to divest the protest movement of its courage or its conviction. The contrary was the likelier outcome. So it has proved. Greenpeace enjoys more firepower than ever in the form of public support, and its

Right: *Police searched the crippled* Rainbow Warrior *looking for evidence while the ship was in the Devonport Naval Base dry dock.* (Gil Hanly)

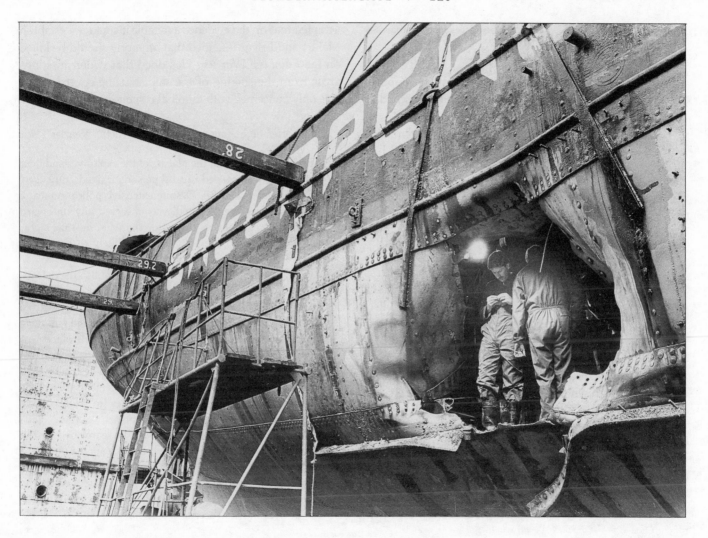

replenished armada is certain to be resolved to embarrass the French.

L'Affaire Greenpeace as it was dubbed by the popular French press after the turn-of-the-century military scandal, *L'Affaire Dreyfus*, was to have its sequel in the courts.

On 4 November Prieur and Mafart faced a preliminary hearing on their charges. Their wait in Mt Eden jail had already been eventful: following rumours that mercenaries were planning to free the pair, Mafart had been transferred to Paremoremo maximum security prison and Prieur became the only prisoner behind barbed wire barricades in Ardmore military correction camp, both near Auckland.

Scene of many famous trials, the old Auckland High Court building was refurbished and turned into a fortress for the hearing. Police went to extraordinary lengths to prevent any breach of security. One measure — a bullet-proof glass enclosure for the accused — was abandoned only after defence lawyers argued this would victimise Mafart and Prieur. About 150 journalists and artists were accredited for the hearing, at least 40 of them from France. News media represented ranged from Norwegian television to the *New York Times* and London *Sunday Times*.

But after these unprecedented preparations for a New Zealand court hearing, the case was over in half an hour. Solicitor-General Paul Neazor, QC, told Judge Ronald Gilbert that the pair had indicated through their lawyers they were prepared to plead guilty to reduced charges of manslaughter and wilful damage. Neazor said the Crown accepted that on the evidence available it could not establish Mafart and Prieur intended that anybody should be killed on the *Rainbow Warrior*. He added that wider questions arose from the sinking of the ship, but the court hearing was only concerned with criminal responsibility under New Zealand law.

In a brief eight-page summary of facts, Neazor said:

There is no doubt that the placing of the explosives and their detonating was carried out by persons trained and expert in underwater warfare. Despite extensive police inquiries, no person has been located who observed any untoward activity in or about the vessel or the wharves that night. Clearly, however, the activities were likely to have been carried out by a number of persons.

The Crown's investigations do not establish the defendants' role in this affair as other than in support of those who actually placed the explosives. As part of their support role the defendants were responsible for picking up and removing from the scene one of those responsible for the placement of the explosive devices. This recovery was made after the devices had been placed and the timers had been set, when one of the persons responsible for the placements then made his way in the Zodiac from the wharves [to] Hobson Bay and a rendezvous with the defendants.

Subsequent to the night's events a search led to the discovery, under Ngapipi Bridge, of the Yamaha outboard motor which had been bought by Andries weeks earlier in London. The Zodiac dinghy was left abandoned at the recovery point. The identities of those who actually placed the devices has not been established.

Mafart and Prieur pleading guilty to the reduced charges was the third setback for the *Rainbow Warrior* crew to coincide with a birthday. On Fernando Pereira's birthday at Mejato Island Steve Sawyer had been severely injured on a shipwreck, the *Warrior* was bombed on Sawyer's birthday, and now it was Nathalie Mestre's twenty-first birthday.

One newspaper headlined its report of the trial: 'The Case of the Century Over in Time for Lunch'. Outside the court, McTaggart claimed it was not 'justice at the highest level' as promised by President Mitterrand. He said: 'I think Mitterrand should have been in the dock today, and Hernu . . . and what'shisname [Pierre Lacoste], the former head of the DGSE'.

A *coup de théâtre*, said astonished French newspaper journalists who were having difficulty understanding the New Zealand legal system. *Le Figaro* said New Zealand was not only France's geographical antipodes; its legal system also belonged to another world. 'The presumption of innocence,' said the paper, 'is contrary to reality.'

Prime Minister Lange rejected claims of political interference, saying the legal system and the prisoners were 'not for sale'. Asked whether Mafart and Prieur would be deported under section 92 of the Criminal Justice Act, Lange retorted: 'Only a lunatic, or a journalist, would ask a prime minister what would be the outcome before they have been sentenced.'

Three weeks later, on 22 November, the Chief Justice, Sir Ronald Davison, sentenced both Mafart and Prieur to 10 years' jail for their role in the bombing. He said the operation was a deliberate terrorist action, carried out for political and ideological motives, and the first offence of its kind in New Zealand.

'The sentence imposed must give a clear warning to such as the defendants and their masters that terrorist-type activities will be met with stern reaction and severe punishment,' Sir Ronald said. 'People who come to this country and commit terrorist activities cannot expect to have a short holiday at the expense of our Government and return home as heroes.'

Watching from the public gallery was Henk Haazen — the only *Rainbow Warrior* crew member among Greenpeace campaigners in the courtroom for the sentencing.

Footnotes to Chapter Eight

1. Henri Hiro, *Tahiti Derrière le Rideau des Fleurs*.
2. The CEP, Pacific Experiments Centre, is the military agency which controls Moruroa and Fangataufa Atolls and oversees the security of the tests.
3. Pascal Krop and Roger Faligot, *La Piscine: les Services Secrets Français 1944-1984*, Editions du Seuil.

CHAPTER NINE

Moruroa, Mon Amour

Mate atu he tete kura, whakaete mai he tete kura.
When one canoe perishes, another takes its place.
— Maori proverb

A CARTOON in *Le Canard Enchaîné*, the French equivalent of *Private Eye*, was strikingly candid. Adam and Eve huddle naked in a Polynesian Garden of Eden as they gaze, bewildered, at a crude H-bomb.

'Look, it's H as in Hernu,' Adam says.

'And as in horror, holocaust, hecatomb and Hiroshima,' adds Eve sourly. It could just as easily have stood for 'Hernucléaire', as Charles Hernu was nicknamed.

To French Polynesians who believed the election of a socialist government in France in 1981 would curb the South Pacific nuclear testing programme, the cartoon wasn't amusing. Nuclear blasts in their backyard is an issue which rankles with many Tahitians who are bitter about the way their once idyllic lifestyle has become hostage to *la bombe*.

When a debonair man with a double-breasted suit trotted off a French Air Force DC-8 at Papeete's Faaa airport for the first time in August 1981, nothing seemed to have changed. Charles Hernu, the hawkish new socialist Defence Minister, could have been any one of his Gaullist or Giscardian predecessors.

Hernu quickly made it clear socialist France wasn't going to curb the tests as had been expected — *la bombe* would be exploded in French Polynesia for a long time yet. Furthermore, he said in a Christmas message in 1982 that France would press ahead with neutron warhead development.

Since then France has announced testing will continue at Moruroa Atoll at least until the turn of the century. Nearby Fangataufa Atoll is also expected to be used as a second Pacific nuclear 'laboratory'.[1]

In its first year of office alone, the socialist Government authorised 11 nuclear tests. France had conducted 115 tests in the South Pacific by the end of 1985 — almost twice as many as the United States in the Pacific region. Seventy-four of the explosions have been detonated underground.

The increasing number of tests is in spite of several disasters since the French nuclear programme changed from atmospheric to underground testing in 1975:

6 July 1979: Two French workers at Moruroa died as a result of an explosion in an underground laboratory. Four others were injured and the blast spilled radioactive plutonium into the sea.

25 July 1979: Part of the atoll collapsed and subsided into the sea three hours after a 140-kiloton nuclear device became stuck in a detonation shaft and was triggered at almost half the usual depth of 800 to 1,000 metres. The blast registered 6.3 on the Richter scale and the subsidence caused a *tsunami* which washed over the island injuring seven people.

March 1981: A storm tore off asphalt covering and flooded a 30,000-square-metre nuclear waste storage area on the northern part of the atoll, sweeping several kilograms of plutonium into the lagoon and into the Pacific Ocean. A trade union report condemning the lack of safety at Moruroa led to an international outcry.

A four-day suspension of tests after President Mitterrand was elected in May 1981 was only a hiccup in the nuclear programme that began in the Tuamotu Islands, 1,500 kilometres south-east of Tahiti, during 1966. (France transferred its nuclear tests from the Sahara Desert to Polynesia when Algeria gained independence.)

'It seems perfectly clear that the only way Tahitians can put a halt to the nuclear spoilation of their paradise — the obliteration of atolls and the slow poisoning of the population — is to become independent,' said Tahiti's best-known campaigner against the tests, Dr Bengt Danielsson. Swedish-born Danielsson and his French wife, Marie-Thérèse, are co-authors of *Moruroa, Mon Amour,* an exposé of the military and French colonial administration in Polynesia.[2]

In the 1982 territorial elections nine pro-independence parties polled only 15 per cent of the total votes between them. However, the largest of the parties, Ia Mana Te Nunaa (Power to the People), won three seats in the 30-seat Territorial Assembly for the first time and are following a strongly anti-nuclear policy. Ia Mana's secretary-general, Jacqui Drollet, attended a meeting of the Socialist International in Brussels during 1983 and distributed a pamphlet about French policies among the 120 delegates. 'When France was chased out of Algeria by the victorious patriots of that country,' the tract said, 'General De Gaulle forcibly installed in our Polynesian islands the nuclear testing centre to which his own people had refused house room in France.'

The progress towards independence made by the Kanaks in New Caledonia has also encouraged many Tahitians. Five Tahitian parties, led by Tetua Mai, who was jailed after setting up a 'provisional government' in Papeete, formed the Maohi Liberation Front in June 1985 with support from Vanuatu.

'If our Kanak brothers are in revolt today it's because colonialist France, without consulting them, grabbed their country,' said Oscar Temaru, the outspoken pro-independence mayor of Faaa, Tahiti's largest town. 'It's because a whole succession of French governments used the country as a human cesspit for 20,000 convicts. It's because the French administration has driven them from their lands to make way for *colons,* who more often than not were freed convicts, or their even-more depraved and brutal former jailers. It's because French and multinational companies have

seized their main natural resources, the nickel deposits of New Caledonia.'

But Tahiti's President, Gaston Flosse, who forced reforms from France in 1984 to give Polynesians a greater say in their government, surprised many Tahitians with his approach to the Kanaks. Flosse signed a treaty — without any constitutional rights to do so — with Vice-President Dick Ukeiwe of New Caledonia, pledging to 'defend their common *French* Pacific interests and promote joint action in political, administrative, economic, cultural and social matters'.

Flosse's neo-Gaullist party, Tahoeraa Huiraatira, rules with 15 seats, backed by three independents. The Opposition is deeply divided. French Polynesia, which became a protectorate in 1847, now has a population of more than 160,000 with almost 20 per cent who are French *métropolitains*. The Chinese community, whose forebears were imported as labourers on plantations, number 10,000. Polynesians and *demis* (mixed-race Polynesians) are clearly a majority, unlike in New Caledonia where the indigenous Kanaks have been turned into a minority in their own land by French immigration policies. (Kanaks make up 47 per cent of the 150,000 population of New Caledonia, which was originally annexed by France in 1853 and turned into a penal colony.)

Left: *A balloon suspending a nuclear bomb above Moruroa Atoll in 1966. Forty-one atmospheric tests were triggered before France began underground tests in 1975. France exploded a further 74 nuclear bombs by the end of 1985.*

The Danielssons and other opponents of the nuclear tests have fears for their effects on the health of Tahitians. 'The same causes produce the same effects and that is why there must be as many radiation-induced diseases in the Tuamotus today, and many more during the next five to 10 years, as there have been in the Marshall Islands until now,' said Dr Danielsson. Atmospheric tests ended in 1974 and in Micronesia it took about 15 years for abnormal health patterns to develop.

The Territorial Assembly in 1981 demanded the suspension of nuclear tests while its own independent commission of inquiry investigated their effects on Tahitians. The Assembly asked for French, Australian, New Zealand and other foreign doctors and radiobiologists to investigate. This has never been allowed.

'Of course, France will do its best to try to block the commission. But the Assembly has been clever this time,' Dr Danielsson said. 'Previous protest moves by local politicians have failed because the French authorities blocked them on the grounds of military secrecy. Now the Assembly is restricting its concern to the health of Tahitians — and how can France quibble over that?'

A sharp rise in the incidence of cancer in French Polynesia has been noted by Marie-Thérèse Danielsson and other researchers. According to some sources there has been an increase in thyroid tumours and leukemia among Polynesians since the tests began.

French authorities in Papeete have refused to disclose health statistics to an internationally sponsored cancer register for the South Pacific. Professor Brian Henderson, of the University of Southern California in Los Angeles, who has collated data from Fiji, New Zealand, New Caledonia, Papua New Guinea and Western Samoa for the register, said authorities in Papeete had also introduced a tumour register but would not disclose details.

Scientists monitoring the cancer rate among Pacific islanders are unable to tell from the sketchy statistics so far gathered whether there is a link with the testing, particularly from the 41 atmospheric tests before 1975. Official information giving the causes of cancer deaths has not been published in Tahiti since 1963 — one year before the Centre d'Expérimentation du Pacifique was established and three years before the first test. The ban has been upheld by Papeete's two hospitals which are run by military doctors.

Most of French Polynesia's cancer cases are sent to France, where they are widely dispersed for treatment in public, private and military hospitals. According to French journalist Luis Gonzales-Mata in *Actuel* magazine, French authorities have been secretly sending large groups of Polynesians on military flights to Paris for treatment of cancer. Fifty Tahitian cancer patients were flown to Paris on one occasion alone. All were aged under 35 and suffering from brain tumours. At the time of the atmospheric tests they were aged between 10 and 20. Gonzales-Mata claimed the records held by the State Secretary of Health's office in Paris showed that 50 patients were sent there in 1976, about 70 in 1980 and 72 in 1981. More than half of them had cancer. When he visited islands close to Moruroa,

Gonzales-Mata found abnormally high incidences of ulcers, miscarriages and stomach troubles.

Charlie Ching, radical leader of Te Taata Tahiti Tiama (Free Tahitian Party), claimed at a nuclear-free Pacific *hui* in Auckland during 1983 that more than 200 Tahitians had died from radiation-linked illnesses in five years. But proving these claims is difficult. Apart from the lack of public health statistics, private doctors have been required to enter the cause of death on a death certificate only since 1983. Autopsies are almost never carried out in Tahiti except in forensic cases. An isolated set of figures released by France in 1983 showed a slight increase in cancer over six years but attributed most of them to alcohol and tobacco.

Many cancer patients not sent to France are flown to New Zealand for treatment, mainly at Dunedin Hospital. They include both Tahitians and Cook Islanders, and French people living in Tahiti. Here is a breakdown of cancer cases brought to New Zealand (provided by the New Zealand Department of Health):

Year	Tahitians	Cook Islanders
1975	10	4
1976	21	4
1977	17	3
1978	19	2
1979	13	26
1980	20	24
1981	36	24

Asked why there were no figures available for the years

since 1981, the chief health statistician, John Findlay, said there were 'long delays' in processing the cancer registrations. Leukemia, the cancer usually associated with exposure to radiation, did not appear in any of the cases. However, without knowing the actual increase of cancer among Tahitians it is difficult to judge what effect nuclear testing has had on the population. Furthermore, the figures for Tahitians are far from complete as they include only those who are referred to New Zealand doctors from Tahiti. Many more Tahitians come to New Zealand each year independently for treatment.

During the Reef and Mankind Congress at Papeete in May 1985 scientists were strongly critical of the lack of information about the poisoning of Mangareva lagoon. Mangareva Atoll is about 400 kilometres east of Moruroa Atoll, and has a population of more than 500 people. During the atmospheric tests it was provided with bomb shelters which were used on more than one occasion, with the islanders' homes being hosed down with water afterwards. Although the fish have been poisoned since nuclear tests began in 1966, American and Japanese toxologists have established that the reason is not that they have been directly contaminated by radioactive fallout.

However, reports by the South Pacific Commission and World Health Organisation do link the increase of ciguatera with the French nuclear tests. The disease is caused by eating poisoned fish which have become contaminated as a result of eating smaller fish feeding around disturbed coral reefs where the ciguatera micro-organism thrives. Symptoms include vomiting, trembling, paralysis and in serious cases death.

Scientists who have studied the cycle that produces outbreaks of the disease believe the ecological changes associated with increases in the ciguatera micro-organisms may be due both to natural causes, such as earthquakes and storms, and man-created factors such as pollution and dredging. Once part of a coral reef becomes infected, the micro-organism tends to spread along the rest of the reef.

According to a SPC study in February 1981, there has been a serious increase in the ciguatera problem in the Gambier Islands. The report said the epidemic was 'preceded by the mass mortality of corals', and that 'human aggression on the living coral environment' was one of the most likely causes. The report didn't specify nuclear tests, but it is believed that pollution and seismic shocks from Moruroa are the cause.

The mayor of Mangareva, Lucas Paeamara, found himself suddenly in the glare of publicity during October 1985. Paeamara had written on 28 August a brief letter to local newspapers drawing attention to cancer and infant deformities on Mangareva, and about ciguatera disease. He wrote:

In the television news of 19 and 20 August various people from the authorities spoke about the Gambier Islands. As they talked about the health of the people under my responsibility, I cannot remain unmoved. This is why I am asking you to publish this letter.

On the subject of cancers: one must mention a few cases investigated by military doctors and also a recent case where the person died because transfer was regarded as too costly. There are babies born with eyesight problems. Another has had defective kidneys . . .

On the subject of ciguatera: it is affecting almost all the fish in the lagoon. There are many fish but they are unfit for human consumption. The many experts who recently met in Tahiti in a conference [Reef and Mankind Congress] could have come here and studied the problem. Some people on the television programme said the population of the Gambiers 'were happy'. How could they be happy knowing that eating fish could be fatal? How can we stop Polynesians from eating fish, their traditional food?

It isn't for me to say what the cause is. I will leave that to the experts who (I think) are studying the disease. But contrary to what some people think, life conditions in the Gambiers are far from ideal.

The lagoon of Mangareva was used to clean out warships and as a dump for nuclear wastes. Although our people have repeatedly asked for medical teams to check our health, this has never been done . . .

The two French-owned newspapers, *Les Nouvelles* and *La Dépêche*, would not publish the letter, but the Tahitian language evangelical paper *Vea Porotetani* did. And journalists in Papeete to cover the peace flotilla's protest off Moruroa gave Paeamara a lot more publicity.

Mayor Oscar Temaru took up the case and managed to get Paeamara's letter published in one of the daily newspapers. The publicity highlighted another reason why the French military were worried by the *Rainbow Warrior's* protest voyage, 'their plan to carry out an informal health survey on Mangareva and other atolls.' Temaru said:

The sad truth is that the only ones who have tried to help us are the Greenpeace ecologists. But was this fear of having scientists poking their noses into the Mangareva mess really a sufficient reason for the French secret service to embark on the risky operation of sending combat divers to Auckland harbour to sink the *Rainbow Warrior*? For we must not forget that the 3,000 French soldiers and foreign legionnaires on Moruroa could easily have repulsed an attack by a dozen ecologists.

We must look for a more convincing motive, which, alas, isn't difficult to find. Greenpeace had planned to include on the *Warrior* doctors and scientists ready to undertake the health survey the Territorial Assembly has been clamouring for since 1981 — and to start it at Mangareva! The ultimate aim of the sabotage was thus to prevent the unpleasant truth from becoming known.

During 1983 an independent New Zealand filmmaker tried to get a visa to make a film about nuclear testing and its impact on Tahiti but was turned down by the then High Commissioner, Paul Noirot-Cosson. The Australian television current affairs programme *60 Minutes* also tried to get permission to film, without success. Yet at least two Scandinavian television crews and other European film groups have been allowed into Tahiti in recent years to make similar documentaries.

A New Zealand filmmaker, Peter Rowell, had to use subterfuge to make a documentary about the peace flotilla and Tahitian independence. Worried that the authorities would confiscate footage for the film — provisionally entitled *Quittez Le Pacifique!* — Rowell told them when he entered Tahiti he was making a documentary about the work of a Maori artist. Rowell and cameraman Barry Harbert did shoot footage of Maori carver Matahi Whaka-taka Brightwell and his 21-metre totara sailing canoe *Haiwiki Nui* before it left for New Zealand via Raiatea and Rarotonga. But what the authorities didn't realise was that Rowell was also filming interviews with Polynesian victims of radioactive fallout.

'Only a handful of Tahitians weren't afraid to talk to us — politicians holding office like Oscar Temaru and people who were already dying from their illnesses and had nothing to lose,' Rowell said. Among radiation victims he interviewed was an old man who worked at Moruroa from 1964 to 1979 who vividly described a tidal wave which injured seven people after part of the atoll collapsed on 25 July 1979.

'He was half-paralysed with no eyes left . . . he had been eating fish in Moruroa lagoon for many years,' Rowell said. A woman, whose husband also worked at Moruroa, spoke of two miscarriages and three babies which lost their skin — 'first-stage jellyfish babies'.

While working on the film, Rowell recorded some of his impressions:

La culture de la Bombe: The French have created a society which is totally dependent on the nuclear war machine. Consumerism hasn't only undermined the fabric of society — it has replaced it. There is a total air of expendability about everything. Everyone drives flash cars and yet nobody really cares. Everything is temporary and nobody has any regard for long-term value.

There is little awareness of the threat to their way of life and traditions . . . The French spend more than $90 million a year here yet in Papeete — population 60,000 — raw sewage is pumped straight into the lagoon. It smells and you're not supposed to swim in it. But tell that to the children as they swelter in the tropical heat. Most of the lagoon is dead already!

Discovered in 1872 by the captain of the British whaler *Matilda*, Moruroa Atoll is the rim of a volcano which became extinct seven million years ago. It is horseshoe-shaped, 30 kilometres long and between three and 10 kilometres wide.

Along with neighbouring Fangataufa Atoll, 40 kilometres south, Moruroa was occupied illegally by the CEP without a lease or land deed, which the Territorial Assembly refused to grant. But after pressure from the French authorities, in 1964 the standing committee voted three to two to cede the atolls to France for an indefinite period. The vote was never ratified by the full Assembly.

By the end of 1981 it was obvious that 46 test shafts along the 23-kilometre-long southern stretch of atoll had brought to reality former chief engineer Claude Ayçoberry's description of Moruroa as a *gruyere* cheese'. Stories in the world's press declared 'Atom-test Island Sinking into the Sea' . . . 'Moruroa, the Unstable Volcano' . . . 'Nuke Waste Swept into Pacific'.

To ease the pressure, a drilling rig was towed to Moruroa to sink test shafts under the lagoon. It was believed that blasts detonated in the centre of the atoll would mean less seepage of radioactive waste into the sea.

'How many more explosions can be made before the atoll collapses?' Dr Danielsson asked. 'Nobody knows for certain. Or cares particularly, for when and if Moruroa goes down, there are 80 more atolls in the Tuamotu group.'

Six National Assembly deputies from the parliamentary defence committee became the first non-military people allowed to visit Moruroa after the international outcry in 1981.[3] They spent two days on the atoll in 1982, but were unable to reach conclusive judgments without technical knowledge. When they returned to Paris, they admitted the visit had been futile and that a team of experts should go to Moruroa.

Polish-born Haroun Tazieff, a renowned vulcanologist who was popular with environmentalists because of his opposition to the French fast-breeder nuclear power programme, was chosen to head the team. He seemed an ideal choice. He had been to Moruroa in 1975 when the first underground test shafts were being drilled on Fanga-taufa. His advice then had been to forget about the atolls and make underground tests in the Massif Central plateau in France.

On his arrival at Moruroa in 1982, Tazieff, now State Secretary for the Prevention of Disasters, was accompanied by two senior Commissariat à l'Energie Atomique officials and five university professors. They made it clear their mission was 'preparatory', to make way for a later, more thorough study which was never done.

Instead, the following year the South Pacific Forum was invited to send a scientific team to Moruroa and Australia, New Zealand and Papua New Guinea agreed to send scientists. Vanuatu, the most outspoken South Pacific country on the issue of nuclear tests, refused to endorse the mission before the study began, saying it would be used by Paris to justify nuclear tests.

Since the team's study (dubbed the Atkinson report after Dr Hugh Atkinson, former head of the New Zealand National Radiation Laboratory) was made public in 1984, it has been dogged by controversy. The report found there was no evidence of significant short-term hazards from testing but several Auckland scientists and researchers for Greenpeace have challenged the report's conclusions.

One of the critics is Auckland scientist Dr Manfred Hochstein, director of Auckland University's geothermal institute. He has written a report challenging some of the findings of the Atkinson study, and French scientists' claim that 'settling', or subsidence, of Moruroa Atoll within the

Right: *French ecologist Brice Lalonde (left) and Greenpeace International chairman David McTaggart on board the Vega during the 1981 protest voyage to Moruroa.* (Greenpeace)

top 100 metres of the limestone layer is negligible and natural. If this were the case, Dr Hochstein said, it would be difficult to explain the slumping on the outer reef on 25 July 1979 when a 100-kiloton device was triggered.

'For this slumping it is more likely that some significant compaction of a plastic layer beneath the limestone took place,' he said. 'Points which indicate that some short-term leakage migh: have already occurred have been cited. Additional testing will probably increase the permeability of other parts of the atoll and leakage will be enhanced in the near future, especially if bores in the lagoon are used for future testing.'

Dr Andrew McEwan, a member of the Atkinson team and now director of the National Radiation Laboratory, was quoted by *Les Nouvelles* as saying Greenpeace was 'just a bunch of amateurs'. He said nuclear testing at Moruroa was quite harmless and he would be prepared to take his family there for a holiday.

'If France is behind the sabotage of the *Rainbow Warrior*,' he said, before the French Government had admitted responsibility, 'then it acted prematurely — it had nothing to fear from Greenpeace.'

Replying in an open letter to the Christchurch *Press*, Dr Danielsson suggested that if Dr McEwan thought the nuclear tests so safe, the base should be moved from Moruroa to Akaroa, on the Banks peninsula, less than an hour's drive from the laboratory. 'We're sure,' wrote Dr Danielsson, 'that the Akaroa natives, many of whom are of French ancestry, will warmly welcome the arrival of about 3,000 *compatriotes* and greatly appreciate the boost to the local commerce . . . such a transfer would entail.'

The bombing of the *Rainbow Warrior* almost scuttled the peace flotilla from New Zealand as well. The fleet was sponsored by local peace groups independently of the Greenpeace movement but they had been relying on the *Warrior* as a mother ship for the voyage. She would supply fresh water and provisions and a vital communications link.

The two smallest boats, *Django* and *Kliss II*, were forced to drop out. This left the 16-metre steel scow *Alliance*, owned and skippered by Tony Still, and the cutter *Varangian* (Alistair Robinson) to join the Greenpeace ketch *Vega*. Both boats were equipped with single side-band radios.

'We're the vanguard for the groundswell of opinion in New Zealand for a nuclear-free Pacific,' said the 35-year-old Still. Crewman Rangaunu Godanovich, 44, an Awanui fisherman, added: 'I'm on this to give my kids some space.'

Becoming the focus of news media attention in the wake of *Warrior's* sabotage caught some of the crew by surprise. Paul Hodson, who turned 20 off Moruroa, said he thought the *Alliance* would have 'just tagged along behind' the *Warrior* which would have attracted all the publicity.

In spite of fears that the seven crew of the flat-bottomed *Alliance* were risking their lives, the scow left on 3 August for Moruroa. But they ended up going to Rarotonga first to change a crew member and make some rigging repairs.

On 17 August good news came. Greenpeace had decided

to send its namesake tug to Moruroa on its way from Amsterdam to the Antarctic. The *Greenpeace*, loaded with a prefabricated West German base camp and equipment, would also try to call at Mangareva and other atolls to gather health information.

'As long as France continues testing nuclear weapons in the Pacific, we will continue our peaceful protests,' David McTaggart wrote in a letter to President Mitterrand and Admiral Pierre Lacoste. He appealed for France to join the five-month moratorium on nuclear tests begun on 6 August by the Soviet Union.

Rainbow Warrior deckhand Bunny McDiarmid flew to Curaçao to join the *Greenpeace* crew. Others had been asked to go as well but, as one crewmember said, 'They're asking a bit much when we've had our ship bombed from under us and our mate Fernando Pereira has been killed.'

The peace flotilla boats were almost besieged with people wanting to help with food, equipment, home brew or just goodwill. Engineers and Boilermakers Union members helped do engine repairs on the *Alliance*. One wellwisher wrote an open 'Song to Mitterrand' which was published in the *Listener*:

> *Alors, tell me, mon cher m'sieu,*
> *What do you keep on testing for?*
> *When la Bombe she makes 'le pouf!'*
> *Does she not make 'le pouf!' enough?*
> *Just how grande must la Bomb be*
> *To give la gloire to la Patrie?*

Meanwhile, the Breeze Sailing Club trust, which operates the 30-metre brigantine *Breeze*, offered to make an independent support voyage and Greenpeace agreed. Owner Ralph Sewell named 51-year-old Jim Cottier, who had been to Moruroa in 1973 on board the *Spirit of Peace*, as captain. Raising funds quickly was a problem; the *Breeze's* rigging needed overhauling for the 9,600-kilometre trip and four-and-a-half tonnes of lead ballast had to be removed from the bilges, melted down and cast as a shoe on the keel to give the boat greater stability. A full-page advertisement was booked in major newspapers which said:

BANG! YOU'RE DEAD!
That's how much warning you'd get if a bomb went off in your backyard. You won't even get time to say 'bye' to the person next to you, let alone your loved ones.

The advertisement asked New Zealanders to write letters of protest against French nuclear testing which the *Breeze* would deliver to Papeete, and to make donations towards the $30,000 cost of the voyage. Trust chairman Jim Mason, a barrister, also sent a circular to members of Parliament and mayors throughout the country, asking them to write to President Flosse, appealing for protection for the peaceful voyage: 'The crews are giving three months of their time to support the policy of a healthy nuclear-free Pacific. Fernando gave his life. Will you give us a letter?'

Among the crew of nine was a veteran of British nuclear testing in the Pacific. Turi Hokopaura, 52, a navy engineer for eight years, was on board the *Otago* when the New Zealand frigate was deployed in the Line Islands during British tests at Christmas Island.

While the *Vega* was being equipped for her fifth protest journey crew changes were made. *Rainbow Warrior* skipper Peter Willcox and deckhand Grace O'Sullivan decided to go, which meant that with Chris Robinson on board as well half the crew were from the *Warrior*. The other crew members were New Zealanders Sue Ware, 25, and Tihema Galvin, a 63-year-old Rotorua *kaumatua*.

The *Vega* left on 24 August, followed by the *Breeze* two weeks later. The *Varangian*, after being delayed at Great Barrier Island and returning to Auckland to pick up *Warrior* radio operator Lloyd Anderson, finally left on 28 September.

'First sight of land after three weeks was Raivavae Island,' wrote *Breeze* crewman Rob Morton. 'We passed close inshore, the ocean swell dropping in the lee for a welcome moment. This was the Austral Islands in French Polynesia and we came under surveillance with a white military jet making low swoops over us every second day.'

In Tahiti, two Pacific women — one a Maori, the other Fijian — were expelled within hours of each other for taking part in a candlelight procession supporting Greenpeace organised by mayor Temaru in Fa'aa. Maori land rights campaigner Eva Rickard and Temaru addressed the rally on 16 September which ended in a minute's silence in honour of Fernando Pereira. A Tahitian Evangelical Church deacon said a prayer. The next morning French authorities served Rickard with an expulsion order. A day later Anna Sovaia from Fiji, who had been photographed by a newspaper at the rally, was also expelled.

Greenpeace and the French Navy prepared for a publicity war. With almost a dozen journalists and photographers, and a television crew on board the *Greenpeace*, French Navy officials invited about 20 journalists to Tahiti as a counter-offensive. They joined the escort vessel *Balny*. Remarkably, there were no New Zealand journalists among either group. In spite of the *Rainbow Warrior* bombing having dominated the news for two months, New Zealand's news media preferred to rely on second-hand coverage from other journalists and news agencies.

Jacques Isnard, one of the *Balny* journalists, wrote in *Le Monde*:

> The presence of French and foreign journalists on board the *Greenpeace* and the *Balny* paradoxically enough is lowering the tension between the ecologists and the French Navy. Each side is anxious to appear in the best possible light to their captive observers . . . For both [sides], this miniature war of the Pacific around the nuclear atolls is primarily a large-scale information battle.

According to Philip Brooks, of the Gamma television news agency, it was the biggest French military public relations exercise since the Indochina War. Each night the *Balny* journalists' hand-written copy was flown by helicopter to

Moruroa where it was typed by a military telex operator and sent to defence headquarters in Paris. Then, 'a second verification' was made before the copy was filed to newspapers and agencies.

The French journalists didn't follow the usual practice of foreign colleagues who, covering crisis events such as the Falklands War, added to their copy: *Submitted to military censorship.*

Here is a composite log of the Moruroa protest I compiled from interviews and ship's records on board the *Greenpeace.*

18 September: (After leaving Panama) Tailed by an unidentified ship — dubbed the 'flying Frenchman'. (Before the tug left Europe, former Danish Foreign Minister Kjeld Olesen, one of two parliamentarians on board, accused French secret agents of following him while he was in Geneva for a conference reviewing the Nuclear Non-Proliferation Treaty.)

19 September: Greenpeace ducked behind Cocos Island to give the shadowing ship's radar the slip. The 'tail' got to within eight kilometres before the *Greenpeace* broke cover and tried to intercept it. But the mystery ship changed course and headed away at speed.

20 September: News of the resignation of Defence Minister Hernu and the sacking of Admiral Lacoste prompted a shipboard celebration.

22 September: The *Vega* became the first protest boat to arrive outside the 12-mile limit around Moruroa Atoll.

The French tug *Hippopotame,* which had harassed the *Vega* in the past, anchored a few hundred metres away.

28 September: The *Greenpeace* crew began building a flotsam raft from timber collected at sea. It became the 'prettiest' member of the peace flotilla. 'Tail' still there.

30 September: Message sent to the French Defence Ministry: 'No need to shadow us. Our mission is a peaceful one. We don't have to hide anything and we are completely open. This is why we offer to inform you daily of our position.' No reply.

1 October: Greenpeace now followed by two ships. One ship moved closer than eight kilometres and turned out to be the French frigate *Balny.* The original 'tail' left.

2 October: A Gamma television crew was harassed and thwarted by French authorities in its attempts to join the ship off Hiva Oa in the Marquesas. The mayor of Hiva Oa, apparently acting under orders from the authorities, banned any boat leaving shore.

4 October: The Gamma crew got on board from the island of Nukutavake — 480 kilometres to the south. Two speedboats ferried them to the 12-mile limit where they were picked up by inflatables from the *Greenpeace.* Tailed by two warships again.

6 October: Message sent to French Prime Minister Laurent Fabius:

We would like to . . . invite you to come on board our vessel during your forthcoming visit to Polynesia in order that we may correct some misconceptions you appear to have regarding our motives and objectives . . . While we are strongly opposed to the testing of nuclear weapons, we harbour no anti-French sentiments and commit ourselves totally to non-violent and peaceful protests against nuclear weapons testing throughout the world — north, south, east and west.

7 October: The frigate *Enseigne de Vaisseau Henry* cut across the wake of the *Greenpeace* and went alongside to lower a Zodiac into the sea. As the inflatable headed for the *Greenpeace*, the warship's gun turrets swung around as if for firing. A helicopter circled overhead for an hour. The letter delivered read:

We remind you that passage through the territorial sea within 12 nautical miles of the surrounding reefs of Moruroa and Fangataufa harbour is temporarily prohibited.

'We've been told of a 30 nautical mile danger zone,' said skipper Jon Castle. 'What's that all about?'

'That's the zone from where we move in to head off ships, that's all,' answered the officer.

'Why are your bloody guns trained on us?'

'Ah, that's what you think? Oh no, we have to move our turrets around to make room for the helicopter!'

As the French officer prepared to leave, Gerd Leipold, coordinator of the Moruroa campaign, reminded him that the accusations carried by French newspapers of Greenpeace having planned an invasion of Moruroa, were false: 'You can see for yourself we have only three Zodiacs on board, not 12. As for the landing craft behind you, it's meant for the Antarctic. The bow is reinforced, but not for ramming you like some people are claiming, but for withstanding ice floes.'

8 October: Gamma was prevented from transmitting news images. The pilot of a Cessna light aircraft which made a rendezvous with the *Greenpeace* to pick up a short-range video transmission was warned by a French Navy plane he would be shot down if he flew below 900 metres. The same day the *Greenpeace* was refused permission to land on Mangareva.

10 October: Log entry: 'We can clearly see the towers of Moruroa and the coconut palms. Three warships with us — two frigates and a workboat. Launched the raft today for the first time — looks wonderful but needs a bigger sail. French Navy confused by it — sends a helicopter to watch and draws all their ships together. And the name? It's now called *Kotahitanga* — Maori for one people, the idea of Tihema Galvin.

A delegation from the *Greenpeace* tried to visit the *Hippopotame* but were barred from going on board. Later, the *Greenpeace* cut across the bows of the French tug in a daring manoeuvre. The *Hippopotame* was forced to go full astern, damaging part of its steering gear.

Right: *The secret weapon so feared by the DSGE— the flotsam raft* Kotahitanga *being filmed by press photographers.* (Brian Latham)

'Do you want some help?' Castle radioed to the tug after it hoisted a distress flag.

11 October: One of the two electricity generators on board the *Greenpeace* broke down. A decision was made to go to Papeete for urgent repairs.

13 October: The *Alliance* arrived and the protest flotilla was briefly together — *Alliance, Breeze, Greenpeace* and *Vega*. Only the *Varangian* was still to arrive. A celebration lunch was held on board the *Greenpeace* before leaving for Papeete. Tihema Galvin joined the *Greenpeace*.

14 October: French High Commissioner Bernard Gerard refused to allow the *Greenpeace* inside territorial waters. Harbourmaster Henri Vernaudon barred the ship from the port of Papeete in the interests of 'security, conservation and good management'.

Skipper Jon Castle replied: 'We are dismayed to learn of your intention to deny us the right of innocent passage in French territorial waters. We are unaware of any activities which justify this response. We have only taken advantage of our right to express an opinion opposed to the tests of nuclear weapons by peaceful protest.'

A request for a reconsideration was refused.

15 October: Ten Tahitians, led by mayor Oscar Temaru, greeted the *Greenpeace* at sea in a fishing boat, bearing traditional gifts of bananas, coconuts, papaya, and shell and frangipani leis.

'We welcome you to Tahiti and want to tell you many Tahitians support what you are doing and are opposed to nuclear testing,' said Temaru, who added many Tahitians had wanted to join the *Rainbow Warrior* before she was sabotaged.

16 October: The *Breeze* arrived off Papeete with a leak and asked for shelter outside the harbour. Refused. Trust chairman Jim Mason flew into the Tahitian capital with his 16-year-old daughter, Katherine, from New Zealand. He hoped to persuade the High Commissioner to relax the ban as the *Breeze* was not a Greenpeace boat. A reception by Temaru in Faaa was planned so more than 300 protest letters, including one from Mt Everest conqueror Sir Edmund Hillary, now New Zealand's High Commissioner to India, could be handed over.

17 October: *Greenpeace* left for Auckland after temporary generator repairs. Mason succeeded in persuading High Commissioner Gerard to lift the ban on *Breeze* — for one hour! But after mooring at Paea to take on provisions and carry out caulking repairs, the boat moved back outside the territorial limit, tacking back and forth for three days. Mason tried unsuccessfully to persuade President Flosse to receive the crew and accept the letters.

20 October: The *Breeze* had a rendezvous with Oscar Temaru and his supporters. But high seas and strong winds prevented Temaru's fishing boat and the *Breeze* from linking up and they were forced to exchange parcels by long poles.

Right: Protesting off Moruroa. From left: the scow Alliance, *ketch* Vega, *brig* Breeze *and tug* Greenpeace. *The other New Zealand boat,* Varangian, *had not yet arrived.* (Pierre Gleizes/Associated Press)

According to an opinion poll published by *Le Matin*, about 56 per cent of French people believed the navy had the right to prevent protest ships from entering territorial waters around Moruroa.

With the *Alliance* also heading back to New Zealand, *La Dépêche* ran a banner headline: GREENPEACE ABANDONED.

Francis Sanford, a prominent Tahitian leader, known as *metua* (father), who had been an outspoken opponent of nuclear tests for 20 years, resigned from the Territorial Assembly and retired from political life.

21 October: The *Varangian* joined *Vega* off Moruroa. Greenpeace coordinator Gerd Leipold told the *Vega* by radio that Fabius and several cabinet ministers would arrive in Moruroa to observe another nuclear test on 24 October. But this time not only was the test being announced in advance, selected journalists were also being invited to witness the blast.

Chris Robinson, considering whether to breach the 12-mile limit, wrote:

> Would we lose the *Vega* for a long time? With the *Warrior* sunk, handing *Vega* over, would we look like losers? Possibility of heavy jail terms or worse. Possible detrimental press — definitely in France. If ever we are going to head for Moruroa, it has become obvious now is the time.
>
> We are capable of hanging out there for a long time; suddenly it has all changed. We sounded things out on the radio. Others joined the decision. The *Varangian*, just arrived, backed us wholeheartedly. It was all on!

24 October: The *Vega* crew prepared to sail directly to Moruroa in a last-minute attempt to stop or delay the test.

'We're fully aware of the risks we face,' Robinson told the *Greenpeace*. 'The test could cause a tidal wave.' Radio Tahiti reported bomb staff would be deployed in the *tsunami* towers on the atoll. Peter Willcox said: 'We're here with only our tiny boat and without any weapon — we don't threaten anybody.'

0100 hours (local): The *Vega* breached the 12-mile limit and headed for Moruroa. Willcox operated the VHF radio to the *Greenpeace* and to Lloyd Anderson on the *Varangian*. Grace O'Sullivan and Sue Ware took turns at the helm.

0120 hours: Warship *Taape* within 300 metres of the *Vega*, flashing lights.

0200 hours: Vega told it was within the 12-mile limit.

0245 hours: Greenpeace unable to hear the *Vega*. Anderson became the radio intermediary; made contact and then lost sight of the *Vega's* lights.

0415 hours: New contact with the *Vega* through Anderson. The *Vega* was now nine miles off Moruroa, travelling at four knots.

0419 hours: The *Vega* was now eight miles from Moruroa and reported a warship 30 metres away.

0438 hours: Willcox reported the *Taape* had hoisted the SQ2 signal — 'Stop or hove to!'

0442 hours: Eight marine commandos with truncheons boarded the *Vega* from a Zodiac inflatable. A French voice called the *Vega* and then silence. 'The bastards have got the *Vega*,' Anderson told the *Greenpeace*. Robinson later recounted the capture as the marines boarded:

> It didn't look like a friendly call. With our wrists bound, Peter and I were delivered to the afterdeck of the *Taape*, Grace and Sue came next. Soon after, we were ushered into the captain's day cabin, hands freed and under guard. The *Taape* towed *Vega* into Moruroa lagoon. They took their time; we knew the test would be that morning.

Two Government ministers, the new Defence Minister Paul Quilès and Secretary for the Prevention of Disasters Haroun Tazieff, hovered in a helicopter above the explosion, codenamed Hero.[4] But they scarcely noticed a ripple in the lagoon.

'It passed the pencil test,' Fabius quipped to reporters after watching the blast on command centre television monitors 20 kilometres away. 'There were three pencils standing upright on the table before me and none of them fell.'

Journalists watching the screens saw the picture blur briefly and then clear to show a pile of sandbags directly above the explosion chamber had not been disturbed.

Although news of the seizure of the *Vega* and crew was broadcast quickly from the *Greenpeace*, Jim Mason and his daughter, Katherine, didn't hear about it until late that night — from Oscar Temaru. Katherine noted in her diary:

> To have a mayor come knocking on your hotel door at 10.15 p.m., pleading for help, is enough to break anybody's stone heart. His face showed the worst despair I've ever seen. He revealed to us, with an expression like a person telling a close friend a relation has died, that the *Vega* and her crew had been arrested. It must have been a bitter blow!

The Masons presented Temaru with a framed photograph of the *Breeze* and prepared to return to New Zealand as the *Vega* crew were taken to Hao Atoll military base. Confusion surrounded the crew's detention because the navy had not been able to find their passports which had been hidden among the yacht's tools. A week later they were deported and the *Vega* was fined. Greenpeace was ordered to pay $8,000 for the release of the *Vega* — but the fine was later dropped.

Footnotes to Chapter Nine

1. Fangataufa Atoll, in the Gambier Islands, was used for the first French thermonuclear test in 1968 and also twice in 1975 for the first underground tests.
2. Bengt and Marie-Thérèse Danielsson, *Moruroa, Mon Amour*, Penguin. Currently being revised with 10 additional chapters under the new title *Poisoned Reign*.
3. The first visit to Moruroa by non-military people was prompted by the *Vega's* third protest voyage to the atoll. On board were David McTaggart, Lloyd Anderson, Chris Robinson and Tony Marriner from Greenpeace and Brice Lalonde of France's *Amis de la Terre*.
4. The Hero nuclear test at 0750 hours on 24 October 1985 had a yield of only five kilotons — by far the smallest all year. Two days later a 15-kiloton device was triggered, followed by a seven-kiloton bomb on 24 November and a 50-kiloton test on 26 November.

CHAPTER TEN

The Nuclear Blackmailers

*Your policy has had only one aim — being able to freely
dispose of our country as a testing ground for your
nuclear weapons.* — Tahitian deputy John Teariki

ON 26 May 1985, six weeks before the bombing of the *Rainbow Warrior*, the sixth French nuclear-armed submarine, *Inflexible*, equipped with 15,000 kilotons of multiple warheads, slipped underwater off Île Longue. It headed into the eastern Atlantic on its maiden patrol. The launching marked a significant step in the French nuclear buildup.

The *Inflexible* is armed with 16 M4 missiles, each with a range of 4,500 kilometres. They are tipped with six 150 kiloton independently targetable thermonuclear warheads (MIRV) — capable of destroying the heart of Soviet industry and most major Russian cities.

Earlier, Redoubtable-class nuclear submarines were armed with 16 M20 single warhead missiles. But they will now be replaced with M4s while a new, more advanced missile, the M5, is being developed. Once all six submarines have the MIRV system, France will have 592 nuclear warheads poised to strike Soviet targets.

The *Inflexible* has been hailed as a triumph of French technology and a reaffirmation by President Mitterrand of the nuclear *force de frappe* that General Charles de Gaulle made the foundation of French military power.

France is the world's third-ranked nuclear power. It is well ahead of Britain — which has also been expanding its nuclear forces — and the two countries now have more than 1,200 nuclear warheads. The United States has repeatedly rejected Soviet demands that French and British warheads be counted as part of the American arsenal, although the two superpowers have been discussing cuts of 2,000 warheads each.

The Soviet Union offered in October 1985 to negotiate with Britain and France over their nuclear weapons, but France flatly said no, and Britain said it was willing to limit its nuclear armoury only if the superpowers first made big cuts in theirs.

France regards itself as a global power. Besides the two superpowers, it is the only nation that maintains a truly global communications and intelligence system, as well as long-range sea and airlift capability.[1] With the declaration of 200-mile exclusive economic zones in the Pacific, France gained control of 11 million square kilometres of ocean, making it the third-largest coastal state in the world.

Part of the credit for the increasing power of the French independent nuclear deterrent is due to a secret diplomatic deal between Washington and Paris. Under the agreement, the United States has provided the most advanced supercomputers to the French nuclear industry, reversing a 16-year-old policy. In return, France is providing greater solidarity with the Western military alliance confronting the Soviet Union.

According to Patrick Sloyan of *Newsday*, the agreement between Mitterrand and Reagan dates from 1982, the year after the socialists came to power in France. In August of that year the first of eight American Cray I supercomputers was delivered.

The Commissariat à l'Energie Atomique, which controls both military and power-supply uses of nuclear energy, put the high-speed, $36 million computer to work solving hydrogen warhead problems which had previously defied French scientists. Later, additional Minnesota-made supercomputers were supplied to French defence research agencies developing a new generation of sea, land and air-launched nuclear missiles. The Cray I can be used for design and simulated testing in aerospace, nuclear reactors and weapons research as well as for code-breaking and, particularly vital for France, for developing the next generation of computers.

Mitterrand has supported Reagan's policies towards Moscow, at times to the surprise of the left wing of the ruling Socialist Party. As part of a resumption of military coordination with Nato, France has established a 47,000-man Force d'Action Rapide (FAR) for fighting alongside Nato and for intervention in Third World countries — including nations in the Pacific.[2] Mitterrand also backed Nato's controversial decision to deploy United States-controlled Pershing II and Cruise missiles in Europe.

French military power in the South Pacific is complementary to United States interests in the region. In fact, American strategy for the South Pacific depends on French colonialism.

The planned French military buildup is centred on New Caledonia. A plan for a giant Subic Bay-style base near Tontouta international airport, shelved by conservatives, has been revived by the Mitterrand Government since Labour was elected to power in New Zealand and the subsequent furore with the United States over the nuclear ships ban. Washington has contingency plans for bases in Belau and the Marshall Islands to back up Guam should the Marcos regime in the Philippines collapse. It also relies on American Samoa and Fiji for support.

A strategic military base in New Caledonia would be the French trump card in its bid for a stake in the vast, untapped wealth under the Pacific Ocean. Following earlier speculation about the plan, Mitterrand confirmed in January 1985 during a brief visit to Noumea that France would build the base with acces for at least one nuclear submarine. He also ordered the military forces in the territory to be substantially increased.

By the time of the territorial elections on 29 September, regarded as a trial referendum on independence, regular forces had been almost doubled to 4,500.[3] This represents one soldier for roughly every 30 citizens. Kanak leader Jean-Marie Tjibaou, who has strong anti-nuclear views, has promised that once the Kanaks are in power he would refuse to host *any* foreign base.

The buildup is part of a three-year plan estimated to cost $42 million and calls for the deployment of 25 Jaguar strike aircraft along with several Transall transport planes at Tontouta. A new base with a 3,000-metre runway and a 300-metre wharf would be built at a nearby deep, sheltered bay and would replace Hao Atoll in French Polynesia as the biggest military base in the South Pacific.

The base would provide an alternative port of call for United States nuclear-armed warships should the South Pacific nuclear-free zone treaty be tightened to exclude such visits. New Caledonia could also provide a staging airfield for United States aircraft monitoring missile tests in the Tasman Sea.

One of the strategic interests to be protected by the base would be French access to New Caledonia's nickel mines where production dropped by more than 40 per cent during 1985 because of the strike over independence. The territory has a third of the world's nickel resources, along with other ores necessary to produce high-tensile metals needed for arms manufacture. (France is the world's third largest arms export and sells to 56 countries.)

Mitterrand has also adopted a policy of close cooperation with the United States in an attempt to prevent the 'New Caledonian disease' infecting French territories in the Caribbean. In the first joint American-French military exercises in the region late in 1985, French marines landed on the Puerto Rican island of Vieques, marking a significant shift in French policies.

Soon after his election, Mitterrand welcomed Maurice Bishop, then leader of the marxist Government in Grenada, to Paris and he supplied weapons to Nicaragua. But three months before the French general election, France embarked on the kind of rapid intervention exercises that prepared United States troops for the invasion of Grenada in 1983. No doubt they would be useful in the Pacific as well.

France fears the spread of *indépendantiste* ideas from the Kanak movement to the French departments of Guadeloupe and Martinique. During April 1985 independence groups from both islands gathered with other campaigners in French-ruled territories for a congress entitled in pidjin *Konferans à Denye Kolini Fwanse* (Conference of the Last French Colony) in Guadeloupe. Kanak delegates played a key role at the meeting.

Mitterrand has also more than doubled the French military presence in the Caribbean possessions from a 3,000-strong garrison to 7,000 troops.

Right: *French Pacific Regiment troops in Noumea. France has embarked on a major buildup of troops in the South Pacific and plans to build a naval base and military airfield near Tontouta International Airport.*

Contrary to United States claims of a Soviet military threat to the South Pacific, an independent report commissioned by the State Department has branded French colonial intransigence and rigid American policies as the main source of instability in the region.[4] The report was prepared by Pacific affairs specialists Dr Robert Kiste, who heads the University of Hawaii's Centre for Asian and Pacific Studies, and Dr Richard Herr, an American political scientist at the University of Tasmania.

It regards the potential for Soviet political and military penetration of the South Pacific as minimal. It also rejects Western suggestions that island nations such as Kiribati, Vanuatu or the Solomon Islands would necessarily be vulnerable to exploitation by accepting more Soviet commercial contact — such as fishing agreements.

'The report shows that while the United States says that the Soviets are the bull in the South Pacific china shop, in fact it is the United States itself and its close ally France who are the bulls,' said Peter Hayes, a researcher for the independent Massachusetts-based Nautilus Research Centre. 'The notion that the United States or Australia or New Zealand can dictate who the islanders will even talk to or trade with is clearly a hangover from the colonial era, now overlaid with the rhetoric of the Cold War.'

Hayes says Washington will pressure Australia to police the region while building up its own presence. (The United States Pacific Command, with headquarters in Hawaii and key bases in the Philippines, already covers half the world — from the Indian Ocean and the Antarctic to the Arctic — and has more than 350,000 military personnel .)

The report concludes that the Soviet Union has been shut out diplomatically in the South Pacific, with ports closed to Soviet vessels since December 1979 as a result of the Afghanistan invasion. It also notes that because the United States, Australia and New Zealand want to keep the Soviets out of the Pacific altogether, rather than seeking to limit their penetration, the Anzus nations tend to exaggerate the dangers of any Soviet contact with an island nation.

'By any rational and objective assessment, it is clear that France has created the greatest opportunities for Eastern bloc penetration ... French attitudes on decolonisation have banked up frustrations which have found outlets in Libya and Cuba.' It says rigid aid practices, import quotas, hardline attitudes over fisheries resources, enthusiasm for nuclear warships and capitalism all generate antagonism towards the United States.

The Reagan administration argues that a United States military presence is required across the Pacific to prevent the Soviet Navy from gaining a foothold. That means continued American hegemony in Micronesia through neocolonial compacts of free association, counter-insurgency in the Philippines, and ostracism for New Zealand and Vanuatu or any other Pacific nation which denies United States nuclear port access. It also means support for the French in maintaining their Polynesian nuclear testing ground and in keeping a tight grip on New Caledonia, lest it become the 'Cuba of the Pacific'.

Much is made of the Cuban connection with Vanuatu and Libyan aid to the Kanak independence movement. In fact, the links are rather tenuous. Vanuatu did receive political support from Cuba in the United Nations during its independence struggle. It is now part of the non-aligned movement and it maintains diplomatic relations with Cuba — through an annual visit by the Cuban ambassador resident in Tokyo! Apart from a brief visit to Libya by two Kanak leaders and later a group of Kanak militants in 1984 — largely political posturing to draw international attention to their independence cause — the Libyans have not been involved.

The United States suggests that while Soviet surrogates (Libyans) engineer insurgencies in New Caledonia, Soviet naval vessels disguised as fishing trawlers penetrate the region, turning the once-placid American lake into a bloody one.

Balancing this, the report by Kiste and Herr says: 'The fact is that in no other major area of the world is the Soviet Union so completely without friends, access or influence'. And while conceding that 'under the right conditions' the Soviets would involve themselves in regional affairs, the authors say current Soviet access has been limited to a minor aid network, which has been largely rebuffed.

On 6 August 1985, the fortieth anniversary of the United States dropping the world's first atomic bomb on the Japanese city of Hiroshima, the leaders of the South Pacific Forum were gathered in the thatched-roof Rarotonga Hotel on the main isle of the Cook Islands for an historic occasion. Eight of the 13 leaders endorsed and signed the Rarotonga Treaty, advocating a regional nuclear-free zone.[5] Another signed a couple of months later and others were expected to sign following ratification by their parliaments.

The pact was the response of some of the world's smallest, most isolated and weakest nations to the nuclear despoilation of the Pacific. It was also promoted by Australian Prime Minister Bob Hawke in an attempt to counter the more radical anti-nuclear stance of New Zealand and Vanuatu. Although New Zealand was one of the signatories, Vanuatu has refused to sign until the treaty is more comprehensive.

The nuclear-free zone prohibits only land-based storage of nuclear weaons, nuclear waste dumping and nuclear tests. Nuclear missile tests may continue and nuclear communications and intelligence bases are allowed. Also, individual countries can decide if nuclear-armed ships and aircraft can use their ports and airfields, and can decide which parts of the nuclear fuel cycle may be developed. Both latter clauses let Australia off the hook.

More than 220 nuclear bombs have been exploded in the Pacific since Hiroshima and Nagasaki — half of them French.[6] From 1946 to 1958 the United States triggered nuclear devices in the Marshall Islands and at Johnston and Christmas Islands; Britain tested bombs at Christmas Island and at three sites in Australia during the 1950s and 1960s. France is the only country still exploding nuclear bombs in the Pacific.

'Populations in Japan, the Marshall Islands and in Australia are known victims of nuclear testing in the Pacific,' said Dr Tony Atkinson, of the New Zealand branch of the Nobel Peace Prize-winning International Physicians for the Prevention of Nuclear War. 'It is highly likely that the people of French Polynesia are suffering serious radiation-induced diseases and they are being hidden by military security.'

A United Nations report estimated that 150,000 people have died or will face premature death as a direct result of nuclear weapons testing in the Pacific by Britain, China, France and the United States.

Since the early 1960s, American strategic missiles, including Polaris, Minuteman, Trident and MX, have been tested at Kwajalein Missile Range in the Marshall Islands. Missiles fired 7,000 kilometres away at Vandenberg Air Force base in southern California splash down in the vast lagoon of Kwajalein Atoll, which is also used for Star Wars research. Once or twice a year the Soviet Union uses the North Pacific to test ballistic missiles, while in 1980 China tested missiles in the South Pacific near Tuvalu.

Thousands of tonnes of radioactive waste have been

Left: *The signing of the historic Rarotonga Treaty, the nuclear-free South Pacific zone pact on 6 August 1985. New Zealand Prime Minister David Lange signs the document. Other Pacific leaders pictured are (from left): Tofilau Eti (Western Samoa), Dr. Tomasi Puapua (Tuvalu), Sir Robert Rex (Niue), President Ieremia Tabai (Kiribati), Ratu Sir Kamisese Mara (Fiji) and Sir Thomas Davis (Cook Islands, partly obscured). Australian Prime Minister Bob Hawke also signed.* (Matthew McKee)

dumped in the Pacific since the nuclear power and weapons programmes began. The Soviet Union has been regularly jettisoning radioactive waste in the North Pacific for some years. France is also believed to dump nuclear waste in the South Pacific and at least two occasions have been documented when deadly plutonium and other radioactive waste has been washed into the sea at Moruroa Atoll during storms. The United States military has repeatedly dumped radioactive waste in the ocean, using Utirik Island in the Marshalls as a dump site for several years.

The United States has been forced to postpone scuttling 100 decommissioned highly radioactive nuclear submarines off the California coast. Japan has been trying to persuade South Pacific nations to agree to it dumping low-level radioactive waste at a site in the deep Marianas Trench, about 1,100 kilometres north-west of the Northern Mariana Islands. The London Dumping Convention in 1983 adopted at two-year moratorium on all nuclear waste dumping in the world's oceans, partly because of lobbying by Kiribati and Nauru. The ban was extended indefinitely in 1985 pending economic, scientific and social studies on the impact of low-level waste dumping.

Australia has about 315,000 tonnes of uranium — nearly 20 per cent of the world's reserves. Exports of uranium destined for power nuclear reactors are likely to be used for the manufacture of nuclear weapons to be tested or deployed in the Pacific. Non-proliferation safeguards are largely ineffective.

Widespread anti-nuclear sentiment in the Pacific is

reflected in a poster which says, 'If it's so safe store it in Washington, dump it in Tokyo and test it in Paris.'

The great ocean surrounding us carries the seeds of life. We must ensure that they don't become the seeds of death,' Tjibaou told trade unionists in a moving speech at the 1982 Pacific Trade Union Forum in Noumea. 'A nuclear-free Pacific is our responsibility, and we must face the issues to live and protect our lives.'

The South Pacific's strongest advocate of anti-nuclear policies and opponent of colonialism, Vanuatu Prime Minister Walter Lini, believes the treaty isn't what Pacific Islanders want. Lini predicts the region's churches and academic institutions will continue agitation for a comprehensive nuclear-free treaty.

If governments are seen to be ignoring the real wishes of the people of the South Pacific, Lini warns, there will be a loss of confidence and credibility in the region's democratic institutions. He told *Islands Business*, 'It is wrong for Vanuatu to sign the Nuclear-Free Zone Treaty. We will make sure that we do not sign a treaty which, as far as we are concerned, is not practical.' Lini said Vanuatu would look at the treaty at the next South Pacific Forum meeting in 1986 and push for a more consolidated approach.

New Zealand Prime Minister David Lange acknowledged the treaty's shortcomings, saying, 'It will never be a perfectly total sort of treaty. It isn't the ultimate.' But, he said, it has signalled the end of nuclear escalation in the region.

Three of the nuclear powers with territories within the nuclear-free zone were formally asked early in 1986 to recognise the treaty by signing three protocols. They are France, which controls French Polynesia, New Caledonia and Wallis and Futuna; the United States, which rules American Samoa; and Britain, which has tiny Pitcairn island as its last Pacific possession.

One protocol demands that they keep their South Pacific territories free of nuclear tests, weapons and waste. The two other protocols require all three powers, along with China and the Soviet Union, to cease nuclear weapon tests and to undertake not to make nuclear attacks — or threaten them — on the treaty signatories.

The stature of the treaty depends on how the five nuclear powers react to the protocols. But by the end of 1985 China alone had expressed cautious approval.

United States' reaction was to sneer. Bernie Kalb of the State Department made a jibe at a Washington press conference, suggesting news of the treaty would arrive by a bottle in the sea. 'I don't know whether the bottle is corked or uncorked ...' Kalb told an interviewer, noting that the treaty didn't back New Zealand's port ban on nuclear-armed warships.

American officials were relieved the treaty had not endorsed the ship ban which was bedevilling New Zealand and United States relations. In January 1985, Lange had refused to allow the non nuclear-powered destroyer *Buchanan* to visit New Zealand after an Anzus exercise because Washington refused to say whether the ship was carrying nuclear weapons.

New Zealand's impertinent stance threatened American strategy for the region and because the country is insignificant militarily it can be sacrificed as an example to more important allies. As the conflict deepened, the Pentagon cancelled joint military exercises and consultations with New Zealand, cut off intelligence information, refused to berth New Zealand ships, and delayed the supply of computer software for New Zealand's Skyhawk jets. State Department officials also threatened that the nuclear ban would 'probably result in termination' of the US-New Zealand mutual defence arrangement.

These punitive actions contrasted with the limited United States response in May 1985 to a similar Chinese refusal to permit American nuclear-armed warships to visit Chinese ports. But they are similar to American attempts to bully the tiny republic of Belau, which adopted the world's first nuclear-free constitution in 1979. However, Washington has ignored the fact that Belau is still part of the Trust Territory of the Pacific Islands administered by the United States while New Zealand is a sovereign nation.

The islands of Micronesia were captured by the United States from Japan in 1944 after some of the bloodiest 'island hopping' battles in the Pacific. Three years later, Micronesia became one of the 11 United Nations trust territories. But the Trust Territory of the Pacific Islands was the only one designated a 'strategic' trust to be administered by the United States. Under the trusteeship agreement signed in 1947, Washington pledged under Article VI to: 'Protect the inhabitants against the loss of their lands and resources ...

The United States had already acted against the interests of the Marshallese: the year before signing the agreement, Washington selected Bikini Atoll for the first post-war series of atomic tests, codenamed Operation Crossroads. The Bikinians lost their home and the Rongelap, Lae and Wotho islanders were evacuated before the tests.

A year after the agreement was signed, the Rongelap Islanders were irradiated for the first time by radioactive fallout from the Zebra test at Enewetak Atoll in May 1948 — six years before Bravo.

Because Congress failed to meet a deadline on 1 October 1985 to pass legislation that would establish a new political relationship with Micronesia, through the compacts of free association, the United States lost its lease on the vital Kwajalein Missile Range. Kwajalein Islanders are demanding more money for the use of Kwajalein and rejected as inadequate a $965,000 rental payment due under the expired lease. In early November, a group of islanders reoccupied several islands in the splashdown area and forced a halt to American missile tests.

The compact is a bargain for the United States. In return for $2,390 million in direct aid and tax benefits over the next 15 years, it provides for indefinite 'strategic denial' — preventing Soviet or any other foreign access to Micronesia. It also assures the United States use of Kwajalein Atoll for the next 30 years.

Estimates put the cost of the pact at slightly less than what the United States would have paid under the trusteeship. Renegotiating the Kwajalein lease is now expected to cost considerably more, but how much is not yet clear.

Another major provision of the compact would be to establish a $150 million trust fund to settle all claims against the United States resulting from the nuclear weapons tests. About $5,000 million worth of lawsuits are pending, filed by 3,000 islanders whose health or property was damaged by the radiation. The fund would generate an estimated $18 million in interest annually, totalling $270 million over 15 years. But for many critics this provision simply means Washington is passing its responsibility to the Marshall Islands Government.

Two of the four Micronesian governments, the republics of the Marshall Islands and Federated States of Micronesia, would gain status as sovereign — though not fully independent — nations. The Mariana Islands established a commonwealth status with the United States in 1976.

Belau, the remaining government, has a constitution prohibiting nuclear weapons, plants and waste. Belau Islanders voted in favour of the compact in a 1984 referendum, but not by the 75 per cent majority needed to permit United States nuclear development there. Belau appears likely to remain a trust territory for the time being, although President Lazarus Salii, who succeeded the assassinated Haruo Remeliik, promised to solve the impasse.

By mid January 1986 his government had signed a revised compact which included a contingency accord that would turn the nation into a major United States military base if Washington lost Subic Bay and Clark Air Base in the Philippines. The pact, if accepted by Belauan voters, would allow construction of a 16-hectare naval base in Malakal Harbour and a 27-hectare air base in return for $300 million in aid.

During 1985, the United States further increased its military and other aid to Fiji, in contrast to the downgrading of aid to New Zealand. It is clear that the United States is counting on Fiji as a pivot for American influence among island nations. A web of aid spun across the region would entangle Vanuatu and reduce the effectiveness of its non-aligned stance.

The unannounced visit of the United States nuclear attack submarine *Portsmouth* in Suva in January 1986 prompted a wave of criticism of the Fijian Government. The 6,900-tonne submarine was the first nuclear vessel of any type to visit Fiji, which two years ago reversed its policy of barring from its ports warships which could be carrying nuclear weapons. A week-long international peace conference had just ended in Suva and the Government was accused of keeping silent about the visit to prevent protests. The president of the Fiji Labour Party, Dr Timoci Bavadra, branded the Government an American puppet.

'The Greenpeace affair has galvanised anti-nuclear sentiment in the Pacific, much of it against the United States,'

Right: *Antipodean perceptions of French policy towards the Pacific as reflected in newspapers and magazines.* (Trace Hodgson/Listener)

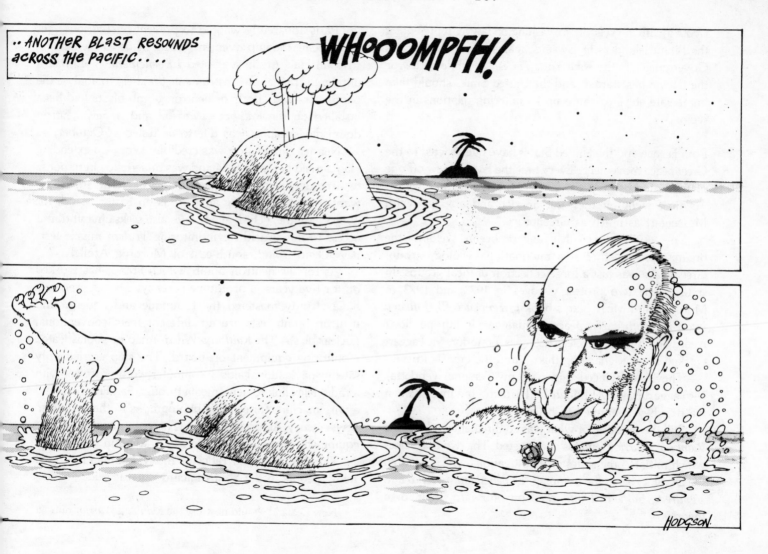

wrote Jonathan Weisgall, a Washington lawyer representing the Bikini Islanders in lawsuits against the United States Government, in the *New York Times*. 'A subtle battle for the Pacific has started, and the United States should take immediate steps to shore up its faltering relations in the region.'

Both France and the United States have overreacted to the Greenpeace movement. 'Every time the French blew off one of those bombs they got angry,' said David McTaggart. 'As time went on they got angrier and angrier.' With McTaggart as much as Greenpeace.

Until 1977, when McTaggart began welding the organisation together as a multinational ecology group, Greenpeace was just a loose collection of local groups. In spite of the two protest voyages in 1972 and 1973 to Moruroa and McTaggart's book *Greenpeace III: Journey into the Bomb*, Greenpeace campaigners in Europe didn't regard South Pacific nuclear testing as a priority. McTaggart worked hard at changing this — and the French knew.

'They're convinced this is all my personal vendetta,' McTaggart said. Although he tried to convince them it wasn't, they continued to believe it.

Still the question of what was so threatening about the *Rainbow Warrior* remains unanswered. The two magazines which initiated the series of investigations which exposed the DGSE's role in the bombing, *L'Evénement du Jeudi* and *Vendredi Samedi Dimanche*, put forward their own theories.

'Paris apparently wanted to prevent overcurious eyes from seeing the improvements being made to the landing strip on Hao Atoll,' suggested *L'Evénement*. *VSD* had a different explanation: 'Instruments that help to analyse the parameters and effects of neutron bomb blasts had been installed on the *Rainbow Warrior*' and 'a new neutron doomsday weapon' was due to be tested in October.

Neither explanation was credible. Work on extending Hao airfield began in 1984 and was undertaken in response to a request from the United States Government which wanted another landing airstrip, as on Easter Island, for its space shuttle. (The United States also seeks aircraft transit access to the airfield for monitoring Trident missile tests near Oeno Island, south-east of Moruroa Atoll.)

As for the neutron bomb, which France has worked on for five years, a prototype is ready. The superpowers have already mastered the technique and underground neutron bomb tests are no different from conventional nuclear blasts. The *Rainbow Warrior* had no sophisticated monitoring equipment on board. The ship carried only satellite navigational aids, a computer-word processor with a radio telex link to news media through San Francisco and a wire machine for sending photographs to the American news agency Associated Press. The only piece of nuclear equipment on board was the $200 radiation detector.

The *Auckland Star* reflected the widespread feeling of many people in the South Pacific when it said:

New Zealand should now use the *Rainbow Warrior* outrage

to shout our message to the world: we don't want a European power that pollutes our environment by testing nuclear weapons on Moruroa; a nation determined to subjugate the rights of the New Caledonian Kanak peoples; a nation so insensitive to a friendly ally that it sends spies and trained saboteurs to disrupt the lawful preparations of a worldwide conservation organisation.

In short the message is simple: with 'friends' like France in the Pacific, who needs enemies? ... New Zealand must catalogue French abuses in the Pacific to demonstrate to the world the true menace, coldly and ruthlessly, France has become to the people who live in this part of the world.

New York Times columnist William Safire, who was Richard Nixon's speech-writer during Watergate, offered some pungent advice to Mitterrand. He wrote:

Stop minimising the original crime. That only focuses more attention on the cover-up. Instead, get furious at the original attack on the *Rainbow Warrior*. Cut out this 'absurd crime' nonsense which smacks of the Nixonian 'third-rate burglary' misconception. Let others talk cynically of the humiliation of being caught — demonstrate that you understand what is *really* shameful, and become incensed at the moral blindness of the plotters.

One of the myths about the bombing perpetuated by the news media was that it had been planned to avoid killing anyone. In fact, it was remarkable that Fernando Pereira was the only person who died.

The suggestion that the first bomb to explode was to be a warning is a gross distortion. It was only by luck that people were not killed by the first blast. The timers on the explosives were set to detonate shortly before midnight, when it was likely several of the crew would be asleep and possibly unable to escape. The first bomb, designed to rapidly sink the ship, was placed on a vulnerable section of the hull beside the engineroom. The second was positioned just forward of the propeller where it would damage the propulsion machinery and steering gear.

Two cabins on the main deck had their floors ruptured by pieces of steel flying from the engineroom blast. By chance, the four crew who normally slept in those cabins were not on board at the time of the explosions. If they had been, they almost certainly would have been killed.

Another question is to what extent did the American secret services provide information about the *Rainbow Warrior* to the DGSE? Both the CIA and MI5 had investigated Greenpeace for infiltration by Eastern intelligence agencies but found no evidence of manipulation.

Early in 1986 the scaled-down New Zealand police investigation concentrated on the role of Colonel Louis-Pierre Dillais and the third team — probably two French navy divers operating under cover with about three mercenaries. The police had sketchy information but it is probable both divers planted the bombs. In Tahiti, there was strong speculation the team could have been landed by a French warship, possibly the *Rubis*.

The exact role of the *Rubis* remains a mystery. The submarine left Noumea and entered the Coral Sea just two days before the *Rainbow Warrior* arrived in Auckland from Vanuatu. Was it on patrol with the specific task of picking up the *Ouvéa* crew if the sabotage operation went wrong?

Admiral Reńe Hugues, commander of French forces in the Pacific, was questioned about this by the Tahitian radio station RTA:

RTA: Admiral, when a boat sinks in the middle of the Pacific, the crew have to swim. Where did they swim to?

Hugues: Some sailors are excellent swimmers. As for how the *Ouvéa* crew were rescued, you're asking me a question I cannot answer. It isn't my area of responsibility. I've no idea what happened.

RTA: The submarine *Rubis* happened to be in the area at the time of the sinking.

Hugues: That day! But in any case, the *Rubis* couldn't have surfaced right beside the *Ouvéa*.

Much is said of France's 'sense of honour'. Yet there was no evidence of it in the *Rainbow Warrior* sabotage. What was shown was a desperate attempt by one of the last colonial powers in the Pacific to hang on to the vestiges of empire by blowing up a peace ship so it could continue

Left: *The French hunter-killer nuclear submarine* Rubis *arriving at Tahiti from Noumea, 22 July 1985. The* Rubis *is believed to have made a rendezvous with the* Ouvéa *and taken off three secret agents. (To protect the identity of the photographer no credit is given)*

despoiling Pacific islands for the sake of an independent nuclear force.

A decade ago, the ecology and anti-nuclear movement developed a following in France as it had in neighbouring countries. However, it was only in France that those beliefs were eroded by a growing delusion — fed by the state — that France's survival depended on the independence of its energy sources, and therefore on the development of its nuclear industry. Perhaps for that reason, the French public reaction to the bombing was as if it were part of a James Bond film rather than a cause for outrage.

The effect on many Pacific Governments, ecologists and peace campaigners has been quite different. Brutally thrust face to face with the reality of nuclear power politics, they have lost their cosy naiveté but their determination to preserve the Ocean of Peace has strengthened.

Footnotes to Chapter Ten

1. Nautilus Research Centre, *American Lake: Nuclear Peril in the Pacific*, Penguin, to be published in May 1986.
2. Like the US Rapid Deployment Force, FAR can call in infantry, paratroopers, marines, and naval and air force transport and local support. The force went into action in Chad in 1983.
3. The Kanak Socialist National Liberation Front (FLNKS) won power in three of the four newly created regional governments and now enjoys *de facto* independence in those areas. Only the Noumea region, where three-quarters of the Europeans live, rejects the FLNKS. Kanak leader Jean-Marie Tjibaou became president of the northern region. A referendum on independence is due by the end of 1987

although defeat for the socialists in the March 1986 elections in France will probably upset this plan.

4. Robert Kiste and Richard Herr, *The Potential for Soviet Penetration in the South Pacific Islands: An Assessment*. Completed in December 1984, the report was not made public until November 1985.

5. Although it has been popularly dubbed the Rarotonga Treaty, its full title is the South Pacific Nuclear-Free Zone Treaty. This zone covers an area of more than 50 million square kilometres ranging from Australia's Indian Ocean territories in the west to an easterr border, beyond Pitcairn Island, that meets a Latin American nuclear-weapons-free zone. It crosses the Equator in some places to cover the Northern Hemisphere portions of Kiribati and extends southwards as far as the Antarctic Treaty zone which is also nuclear-free.

6. The tally of nuclear tests does not include testing in Australia or China although both are regarded as having some effect on the peoples of the Pacific region.

Epilogue

MAUREEN FALLOON watched the television news clip in London after the bombing of the *Rainbow Warrior* and in spite of the shock she couldn't help noticing the paintwork. The striking rainbow curving across the ship's green hull was glowing; it had been painted that afternoon. But by the time Falloon, Greenpeace's international marine division director, saw the *Warrior* in Devonport Naval Base drydock six weeks later the paintwork, like the ship, was lifeless.

The last rites of the *Rainbow Warrior* were painful and drawn out. Even though I had been on board for only three months, it was devastating to set foot on deck again after the sabotage. A hole the size of a dustbin lid had been cut into the buckled floor of my old afterdeck cabin, on the port side opposite Fernando Pereira's cabin, so the damage caused by the second bomb could be more easily inspected.

She was now a corpse. Her soul had moved on; her anti-nuclear struggle now embodied in the peace flotilla and beyond. Her crew was scattered around the world.

'Everyone who has dealt with her over the past eight years considered her a living entity, with a life and a spirit of her own,' Steve Sawyer said. 'That spirit has now passed on, and we would like to give her hollow shell a decent, honourable and respectful burial at sea in honour of what she did and what she once was. The only other alternative is to cut her up for scrap — something none of us could bear to witness.'

Yet even in death, the *Warrior* unleashed powerful emotions and creativity. Schoolchildren painted pictures of the stricken ship, donations poured in in the hope of patching her up, fund-raising concerts were organised and exhibitions put on show.

In Amsterdam, Pereira's family was given an undisclosed sum by the French Government as compensation. But his divorced wife, nurse Joanne van den Boomen, wasn't satisfied with the apology. Defence Minister Paul Quilès wrote:

Madam ... The investigations ordered by the French Government show that the *Rainbow Warrior* was sunk by French agents. On this occasion, Mr Pereira, the father of your children, Marelle and Paul, unfortunately met with his death. The French Government expresses its deep regrets for the deplorable consequences of an act it condemns.

Van den Boomen had earlier demanded that the people who gave the orders for the sabotage and the agents who did the job be punished. She had written to President Mitterrand saying, 'It is scandalous that those who gave the orders and those who carried them out have not been brought to trial. Anyone who imagines that these subordinates could be cleared by making us believe that an order is an order reduces them to the level of robots.'

France also agreed to compensate Greenpeace and negotiations were begun to decide the amount. Washington attorney Lloyd Cutler, former president Jimmy Carter's senior legal advisor, headed a team of lawyers preparing the damages case against the Government.

On Mejato, in the Marshall Islands, the Rongelap Islanders evacuated by the *Warrior* struggled to build a new village and provide themselves with food. An American journalist visiting Mejato with doctors from the Brookhaven National Laboratory towards the end of 1985 reported the medical team was 'prepared for the whispering campaign, but not for the conditions on Mejato, a dry coral reef where food is scarce, the soil is bad and many of the people suffer from diabetes and other diseases ...' Early in February 1986, *Warrior* crew members Henk Haazen and Bunny McDiarmid were expected to return to Mejato to work with the islanders.

Davey Edward joined the *Greenpeace* as an engineer on the Antarctic expedition; Peter Willcox planned to write a book on his experiences as skipper of the 'R Dub'.

Many people who had never cared much about the issues Greenpeace was fighting for suddenly became concerned. The *Rainbow Warrior* was now *their* ship, they believed. How dare Greenpeace decide her fate without their participation! This attitude posed serious problems for the ecology movement. Whatever it decided to do with the *Rainbow Warrior*, it was bound to draw an antagonistic response from one group or another.

At first, Athel von Koettlitz and Falloon explored the possibilities of repairing the *Warrior*. But the costs were prohibitive. Quotes began at $700,000 for hull repairs alone. A replacement ship would be far cheaper. Towing the ship to Singapore for repairs was also ruled out; it would cost $80,000 for the towing.

The longer the police investigation continued, the more Greenpeace investigated other alternatives; burying the ship at sea beyond the 12-mile territorial limit (favoured by most Greenpeace supporters), carving her up for scrap, or turning her into a floating or shore-based peace museum. But while there were plenty of suggestions, no proposal with a realistic financial plan was put forward.

When Carol Stewart and Judy Seaboyer flew to London for the organisation's annual council meeting, they had only one serious proposal to consider. The NZ Underwater Association's president, Allan Fowler, had offered to turn the ship into an underwater memorial for divers. The

Greenpeace council made a unanimous decision on 29 September 1985 to agree to the scheme providing it met stringent criteria such as the approval of local people, it was not detrimental to fishing or the environment and there was no risk of the ship being vandalised.

'The *Rainbow Warrior* will become a haven for the marine life she campaigned to protect,' said Greenpeace International chairman David McTaggart. 'Nobody in the organisation could bear to see her cut up for scrap, but undertaking to repair her is a huge job which is beyond our means. A decent burial at sea is the only honourable end for this ship that served so well on so many campaigns for so many years.'

However, the site chosen by the underwater association — off Slipper Island, Coromandel — was quickly scuttled. The Ngati-hei subtribe, the tangata whenua (local people) of the area, opposed using the site because of sacred burial grounds on the island. A meeting of the Hauraki District Maori Council vetoed the idea.

At one marae meeting, the crew were challenged over the ship being stripped of parts for scrap. If the ship was regarded as a 'body', surely this was a sign of disrespect? Sawyer replied parts that were useful for a new ship were being salvaged and other parts were being stripped so the ship would not pollute the sea.

And did the North American Indians, source of the legend of the Warriors of the Rainbow, agree to the sinking of the ship? The prophecy by an Indian grandmother, called Eyes of Fire, saying the warriors would save the earth was described in a booklet co-authored by an *Inuit* (Eskimo) and a white ethnologist. A copy of the book sank with the *Rainbow Warrior*.

The legend emerged after white settlers first arrived in North America. It foretold a time when white people poisoned all the rivers, and slaughtered the animals, birds and creatures of the sea. When that time came, the Warriors of the Rainbow would arrive to save them.

'We don't pretend to be those people that the legend foresaw,' Sawyer explained. 'We merely believe that the times predicted in the legend are upon us, and appeal to the spirit of all people of all races and nationalities everywhere to come together in the spirit of the legend. Then we will peacefully take up the fight to overcome the forces that would destroy Mother Earth, also known as Gaia, and the Great Turtle of indigenous North Americans.'

The *Warrior* symbolised hope. The rainbows on the hull arched over the dove of peace portrayed many nations and races coming together for peace. The logo on the smokestack was given to Greenpeace on the Amchitka voyage by the Kwakiutl people on the coast of British Columbia as a totem of great power which brought good yet also held danger.

'We have tasted the power in the past,' Sawyer said. 'And now we are grieving over the evil it may bring.'

A day after the Slipper Island burial was ruled out, Dover Samuels, a Maori fisherman and entrepreneur from the remote and beautiful Matauri Bay in Northland, offered to sink the *Rainbow Warrior* off the nearby Cavalli Islands.

'Something came into my spirit that inspired me to do it,' Samuels said later. A former Surfers Paradise restaurant owner and an underwater cameraman for a television documentary on great white pointer sharks entitled *Blue Water — White Death*, Samuels believed the nuclear-free campaign made sense to his people. 'What Greenpeace and the *Rainbow Warrior* stand for is similar to what we Maoris believe: aroha to all mankind, protecting life on our planet and trying not to pollute our environment.'

Apprehensive about offending another group of local people, Sawyer and Stewart drove to Matauri Bay to discuss the proposal. They were warmly received on the marae.

A Matauri Bay clergyman spoke eloquently of when the Reverend Samuel Marsden first stepped ashore there in 1814, an event honoured by a flaking wooden church. He believed the scuttling of the *Warrior* to be the completion of a 'trinity of peace': the arrival of the first Maori canoe in Aotearoa, the coming of the missionaries and now the burial of a peace ship.

Samuels explained how the 'living reef' created by the *Warrior* would help rejuvenate fisheries in the area which had been plundered by trawlers; Sawyer described the ship's campaigns and the evacuation of Rongelap Atoll. The marae decided unanimously for the ship to be buried offshore.

On 5 January 1986, a rock festival was staged to celebrate the burial of the *Rainbow Warrior* about 500 metres west of Motutapere Island, in the Cavallis. But the festival went ahead without the ship. The New Zealand Government, facing a hitch in negotiations for a $20 million compensation claim against France, ordered the *Warrior* to be held pending a possible public inquiry into the sabotage. A good bargaining lever.

In Vanuatu a former island trading boat, *Semle Federation*, was sunk in Port Vila harbour as an underwater landmark in tribute to the *Rainbow Warrior* and environmental work by Greenpeace.

Dover Samuels carried on with preparations to mount the ship's three-tonne propeller as a memorial on Piki-Piké -Matauri, the hill at the northern end of the bay overlooking the burial site. And, as Greenpeace awaited the ship's release, a welder etched an epitaph into a steel plate over the funnel: 'GO IN PEACE RAINBOW WARRIOR'.